BLACK VETERAN
ENTREPRENEUR: VALIDATE
YOUR BUSINESS MODEL,
BUILD YOUR BRAND, AND
STEP INTO YOUR GREATNESS

John,

Thanks so much for supporting
my first book. It's an honour to
have you in my corner.

— "IRON" Mike

BLACK VETERAN ENTREPRENEUR:

VALIDATE YOUR BUSINESS MODEL, BUILD YOUR BRAND, AND STEP INTO YOUR GREATNESS

"IRON" MIKE STEADMAN AND
ALANA M. ABERNETHY

NEW DEGREE PRESS

COPYRIGHT © 2022

"IRON" MIKE STEADMAN AND ALANA M. ABERNETHY

BLACK VETERAN ENTREPRENEUR:
Validate Your Business Model, Build Your Brand,
and Step Into Your Greatness

ISBN   979-8-88504-986-3 *Paperback*
          979-8-88504-987-0 *Kindle Ebook*
          979-8-88504-989-4 *Ebook*

Superheroes do not exist, but you do!

CONTENTS

FOREWORD

Mike and I were like oil and water when we first met.

Why was that? All these years later we still don't know, but what I love is how we still bring it up from time to time and laugh about it.

See, we met at the Naval Academy Preparatory School in Newport, Rhode Island, in the summer of 2005. We were youngins then. I think both of us were hot heads in our own way and ready to answer any challenge that came our way. That challenge happened to be each other a lot of the time, and round and round it went.

Interestingly enough, one of my main memories of us getting underneath each other's skin was during an English class we had together. How cool that here we are now, writing this book together.

Looking back, I know I didn't have any reason to be getting on him. What did we argue about? I couldn't even tell you now, but man, did it seem so real and so important then.

That was our beginning, seventeen years ago, at the writing of this book.

Fast forward ten years to our five-year reunion from the Academy. At the time I lived in Annapolis, where the Naval Academy is located, and Mike reached out before the reunion to see if he could stay with me in my spare bedroom while he was in town.

Without hesitation I said, "You know it!"

Needless to say, but I'm saying it, our interaction had gotten better during our time at school, and after school it was nothing but love. Also, through years of social media, I started to see all he was doing with Fighting Mojo and how he was really out there grinding, trying to help and uplift others with his brand.

I was beyond impressed.

I could tell he had grown as a person, just like I had. Also, he was a classmate, so that is an automatic, "Whatever you need."

We celebrated our five-year reunion that weekend with some of our classmates, and it was amazing. It's wonderful to see how people grow. But the most special moment to me was sitting around with Mike before we'd head out to events and picking his brain about what he was doing. Seeing his passion for and fearlessness in the grind was profound. It was clear he didn't have all the answers, but he was willing to figure it out and wasn't going to stop until he did.

His mind was set.

I was blown away. But most importantly, I was inspired. That conversation planted a seed within me that I could do this too. He never shied away from stating how tough it was and that there were times he didn't know what the next steps were, so I wasn't just thinking because he can do it I can do it.

It wasn't *that* simple.

It was that he had already paved some of the way. And I knew if I needed help and wanted to get where he was, he would help me without question.

I can't really remember, but either before he arrived or while he was there, I bought my Fighting Mojo shirt, which I still have and workout in. I went to his IRON-BOUND Boxing Academy opening in Newark, New Jersey. I donated during his opening, and every month I make sure I donate the amount that will cover the cost of one of his boxers. I do this because:

I believe in Mike.
I believe in what he is doing.
I believe in his vision.
I believe in Mike.

We went from couldn't stand to be in the same room together when we were hot headed youngins to Mike being what I think of as *the* example of a Black veteran entrepreneur.

When he asked me if I wanted to write a book, I hit him with, "You know it!"

The things he has taught me over the years have been invaluable, and what I learned writing this book with him is priceless.

I know you will think the same as you read this book and most definitely as you finish it.

Visit www.BlackVeteranEntrepreneurs.com/Photos see our throwback through the years.

Alana M. Abernethy
Coauthor

INTRODUCTION

"So our people not only have to be re-educated to the importance of supporting Black business but the Black man himself has to be made aware of the importance of going into business. And once you and I go into business, we own and operate, at least the businesses in our community, what we will be doing is developing a situation wherein we will actually be able to create employment for the people in the community."

—MALCOLM X

When I walk into business conferences, entrepreneurial meet ups, and workshops for business owners and notice the absence of Black veteran entrepreneurs (BVEs), I think to myself it is a missed opportunity for them and for our country.

As a proud Black Naval Academy graduate, prior Marine Corps infantry officer turned entrepreneur, living in the heart of Newark, New Jersey, I see firsthand that BVEs are the best equipped and positioned group to address some of our nation's most significant challenges in the Black community.

That the Black community faces an uphill battle in most arenas from an economic and social standpoint is no secret. The struggle in the entrepreneurial arena was compounded in the wake of the financial devastation Black-owned businesses experienced during the COVID-19 pandemic.

According to a 2021 report by the House Small Business Committee, "Black-owned businesses declined by 41 percent between February and April 2020," and those that didn't shut down are still recovering, including many of you reading this book.

For this reason, I believe as Black veteran entrepreneurs (BVEs), we represent the greatest untapped resource we have in America today, because when we rise, we take our families and communities with us.

I know how much you love your country and your people, and they're counting on us.

For the last several years, I've immersed myself in the veteran entrepreneurial community, attending conferences and events, and building an amazing network of veteran entrepreneurs all across the country. I've met BVEs working on tech startups, small businesses in their local communities, and even launching their own venture capital firms, the majority of whom have goals to impact the Black community that extends well beyond monetary returns.

I've also had the privilege of judging multiple pitch competitions for the veteran community. More often than not, I've noticed BVEs launch ventures to support their Black and veteran communities.

BVEs launching community focused ventures isn't only something I've noticed. Syracuse University's Institute for Veterans and Military Families reports that over 40 percent of Black veteran entrepreneurs start ventures to improve society and help the community.

Our passion for serving and willingness to use entrepreneurship to bring about positive change is something we must cultivate and pass along to present and future BVEs.

When I started my entrepreneurial journey in 2016, building a free boxing gym for Newark's youth and young adults, there was no playbook specifically for BVEs. Much of the content I came across surrounding military veterans focused on war stories or the process of transitioning from active duty into civilian careers, not into entrepreneurial pursuits. Additionally, most business literature I found lacked agency for Black Americans, not to mention BVEs.

I found very few books written by us and for us on how-to start local nonprofits, small businesses, and resource guides for overcoming racial bias with regards to access to capital. Over the last six years alone, I've read and listened to well over three hundred business books, and unfortunately I can count on one hand the number of them written by Black authors, none of which were BVEs.

In the words of Toni Morrison:
If there's a book you want to read,
but hasn't been written yet,
then you must write it.

Even now, in the thick of my own entrepreneurial journey, I'd love to find and read a playbook from someone who understands why it's so crucial for BVEs to succeed. So I'm stepping outside of my comfort zone and bringing the vision to life myself, with a book specifically for us and those in our corner.

With all the talk surrounding racial equity and promoting free enterprise in underserved communities, we're uniquely positioned to promote economic growth through entrepreneurship and innovation with the intent to improve the quality of life for Americans, particularly those in underserved communities.

We already have the courage to protect and defend our country. Now it's time to channel that energy into free enterprise to build up our communities. In the following pages, I show you how.

Black Veteran Entrepreneur: Validate Your Business Model, Build Your Brand, and Step Into Your Greatness is your step-by-step playbook for launching your successful venture from the ground up.

I share the best tools, frameworks, and resources that have helped me over the years in order to empower you with what you need to survive and thrive. Don't just read it—implement it, think it, and asks how you can do it better. I hope you come back to this book again and again, and know that no matter how challenging your entrepreneurial journey may feel, you have a playbook to guide you along the way.

1

BECOMING "IRON" MIKE

"The man who views the world at 50 the same as he did at 20 has wasted 30 years of his life."

—MUHAMMAD ALI

I wasn't always "IRON" Mike.

I grew up in Tyler, Texas, a kid with little to no confidence yet capable of more than I knew at the time. My mother, Willeen Steadman, a special education director for several Texas school districts, raised me and my sister. She and my father split shortly after I was born, and to this day I've never met him. I grew up watching my mom raise two kids on her own with the support of friends and family while working multiple jobs, including the front desk at the YMCA a few nights a week.

We didn't live the most glamorous life. As I look back, I can't help but appreciate my mom's sacrifice and acknowledge that, as challenging as things may have been, I never laid my head down at night without a roof over my head or food in my stomach. My mom did whatever she had to do to make sure we were provided for, even if it meant pawning our electronics or borrowing from friends and family, to cover groceries.

My family rallied around to support us, ensuring they were a village for us children, especially my mom's younger sister, Bettie Mitchell, who I affectionately call Aunty Betty.

I wish I could say my childhood experience was unique. I knew I was living a mirror image of other young Black males my age, raised by our mothers, grandmothers, and many other women who, more than anything, wanted for us to stay out of trouble, go to college, get good jobs, and raise our own families. To some these are simply milestones, but in our realities you're fighting gravity, surrounded by drugs, gangs, and teen pregnancy traps. I'm not saying all Black males grew up in a home and environment like me, only the majority I personally came across did.

I didn't grow up hearing the term "entrepreneurship," "venture capital," or any of the standard business lingo. My whole childhood I witnessed my mom and others living paycheck to paycheck.

I wanted something different.

By the time I got to high school, I looked toward the military, first by way of enlistment, but my mom was adamant about me going to college. She fought tooth and nail for me to have the opportunity to attend college. I felt if I didn't at least try, I'd be disrespecting everything she had done and sacrificed to give me options in my life.

One day while sitting in my sophomore English class, I came across the United States Naval Academy. A fellow student had a brochure in his hand and let me take a look. When I saw that you could go to college and also enter the military after graduation, I felt like the Naval Academy was the best of both worlds. I could live up to my mother's dreams for me and also do what I wanted.

From then on, I was determined to attend the Academy. My mom and I sat down and came up with a plan for the next two years. I took the SAT six times, lost fifty pounds, and worked with tutors at Texas A&M, the local university. From anyone looking in, it was a long shot for a kid with a 2.4 high school GPA and no strong track record of athletic or academic success.

The Academy took that long shot. I received my acceptance to the Naval Academy Preparatory School (NAPS) in Newport, Rhode Island. The Naval Academy Admissions board sends students to NAPS to give them an extra year of academic or athletic preparation before they enter the Naval Academy in Annapolis to ensure they have the highest chance to succeed. I earned the necessary grades needed to receive an official appointment to the Naval Academy the following year.

Every midshipman, a term used to describe students at the Academy, is required to participate in a sport at the Academy. Freshman year I chose boxing after taking an introductory class where the head boxing coach, Jim McNally, required us all to spar. That class was my first introduction to the sport that would become a cornerstone of my life, of my identity. I was obsessed, to say the least. Up until that point, all I knew about boxing was what I saw on the television screens. The *Rocky* trilogy stuck out to me the most from what I saw of boxing. From watching those movies, I internalized the story of the underdog fighting his way to the top, becoming a champion through sheer grit.

That story resonated with me so much because I felt like an underdog myself while attending such a prestigious institution as the Naval Academy.

I struggled academically, had low self-confidence, and carried around a chip on my shoulder. Also, because there weren't a lot of Black midshipmen at Annapolis, the school felt void of the Black culture I was accustomed to growing up with in Texas. The list of reasons I felt out of place seemed to grow every week.

I, of course, always knew I was Black, but for the first time in my life, Annapolis's lack of color shoved a mirror in my face. Having that mirror in my face showed me every day what I didn't see around me. I began to question the world around me, including why I saw more Black people working as cooks and in the service department than I ever did in uniform.

And in addition, on the surface, everyone seemed to be more privileged than I was, and it made me uncomfortable and insecure. Especially in the athletic arena. See, I wasn't a recruited athlete, like the majority of the other Black midshipmen. So even with the people I felt I should feel a sense of belonging, I was still on the outside. I'd never been known for any sort of athletic prowess, but something about the ring spoke to me, so I gave it a try.

The first day of training, Navy's head boxing coach, Jim McNally, taught me, along with around sixty other midshipmen, the basic boxing stance and a select few combos. Shortly after, he told us to find a partner who was approximately the same weight and size and prepare to spar for three rounds.

I was baffled. How could he force us to spar so soon?

Next thing I knew, I found myself trading blows for the first time with a classmate. The adrenaline rush was surreal and something I'd never experienced before. I was terrified but exhilarated at the same time. Once we were done, I knew this was the sport for me. I wanted to master it.

Over the course of the next four years, I'd earn three national championships, two Most Valuable Boxer awards, and became captain of the Navy boxing team and graduated with the coveted Zembiec Award in acknowledgment of fallen Marine Corps Wrestler Doug Zembiec, an award given to a graduating midshipman in recognition of indomitable warrior experience exhibited through sport.

Also, that chip on my shoulder during those four years? I brushed it away.

My journey wasn't exactly sunshine and rainbows, the triumphant arc of the underdog that's perfectly wrapped up in an hour and half movie. Academically, I wasn't the strongest student, so I spent hours working with tutors to stay afloat. I failed multiple classes, requiring me to give up my summer and attend summer school. During my sophomore year, my mother suffered a life threatening hemorrhagic stroke, leaving her permanently paralyzed on the left side of her body and requiring twenty-four hour care. Any feelings I had before of being an underdog were amplified once my mom suffered a stroke. It's one thing to deal with the rigors of the Naval Academy. It felt like an entirely different beast with an ailing parent.

Thankfully I had my friends and Navy boxing teammates to lean on. Without them, I don't know if I would've made it.

My experience of boxing at the Academy gave me the grit and mental toughness I lacked as a kid. It also paved my road to IRONBOUND.

As a Navy boxer, I spent time training and sparring in inner-city gyms in Baltimore, DC, and New York City. These gyms were full of Black and Brown kids who looked like me. I felt more comfortable in those gyms than I did at Annapolis. The gym served as an escape and outlet for Black youth, keeping them off the streets and out of trouble. Unfortunately, many of them felt like their only option was to turn pro or turn toward life in the streets selling drugs and engaging in other forms of illegal activity.

This stuck in my head. I vowed to start a gym, similar to the one at Annapolis, that focused on developing young athletes in and out of the ring.

I felt a calling to help other young Black men and women.

During the summer of my sophomore year, the Naval Academy sent me to Newark, New Jersey on a summer internship to teach leadership at St. Benedict's Prep, a private all boys school that focused on young men of color. It was the perfect place for me.

After that internship, I knew that calling would be my life's work. Little did I know at the time that St. Benedict's Prep would again be a part of my journey.

NOT "IRON" MIKE QUITE YET

Through my own grit and the support I needed from friends, professors, and coaches, I graduated from the Naval Academy in the class of 2010 and was commissioned as an infantry officer in the United States Marine Corps. Over the next five years, I deployed to Afghanistan, Japan, and the Philippines. My journey in the Marine Corps also wasn't without its fair share of bumps and bruises.

As a Marine, I was shot at, mortared, and relieved of command for a botched combat operation I led in Afghanistan, but that's for another book. After the botched operation, I spent a little under a year in officer purgatory, filling staff billets where the Marines put officers they don't know what to do with. And then an opportunity arose for me to redeem myself. I rejoined my previous unit that I deployed with, 1st Battalion, 8th Marines, out of Camp Lejeune, North Carolina, my first and only unit I served with during my time in the Marines. You'll have to listen to my podcasts, *Confessions of a Native Son*, or read my next book to learn more about my time in the Marines.

I spent the better part of ten years of my life, from the time I was in high school until I graduated from the Naval Academy, preparing for a career in the military. The military was all I knew and all I had considered. As I looked toward a new future and prepared to transition out of the Marine Corps, all I thought about was boxing and starting a free gym.

Like so many veterans looking toward the next phase after a life of service, I was torn between the safe route, going to graduate school, pursuing a career in corporate America, or following my passion.

After graduating from a prestigious college, serving my country nobly in the military, and feeling I did everything I was supposed to do, I chose to follow my passion.

I would build a free boxing gym somewhere in an inner-city. I remember telling myself, "I've done everything I was supposed to do up to this point. Now it is time to follow my passion."

Having spent multiple summers interning in Newark at St. Benedict's, I chose to relocate to Newark. I'd fallen in love with the city and had always contemplated coming back to coach boxing at some point. Growing up I didn't know there were private schools that catered to Black males, so when I came across St. Benedict's for the first time it planted a seed in me. I knew it was the place for me.

Once I completed my five year service obligation to the Marine Corps, I relocated to New Jersey. I accepted a job at St. Benedict's Preparatory School, serving as the residential housing director, living on campus with more than seventy teenage males.

And so I began my entrepreneurial journey.

I arrived in town and began coaching boxing to the kids at St. Benedict's. I didn't have a boxing gym, so I'd drive the few kids I'd recruited around town to train at different gyms, paying out of pocket for them to train. We also used the dormitory, pushing tables and chairs out of the way, to practice.

Shortly after I arrived in the city, I had a chance encounter with Obalaji Baraka, known around town as OB, the manager of recreation for the city of Newark, at an outdoor boxing match. I approached Obalaji and asked about outfitting a space in the city for a free boxing gym. I told him my ambitions for running a program similar to my experience at the Naval Academy, where we had uniforms and camaraderie, with the ultimate goal of training young athletes not to become professional boxers but to graduate from college and contribute to society in a positive way.

After some back and forth, I eventually got the thumbs up from OB and the city of Newark to build a boxing gym in the back of a leaky recreation center in the Ironbound neighborhood of Newark. I'll never forget the day he first showed me the gym, along with my partner, Keith Colon, whom I met at a local boxing gym around the same time. Keith was getting out of prison at the time I left the Marines and training his son at the same gym where I coached. Keith and I are kindred spirits, and we've been attached at the hip since the day we met. OB picked me and Keith up in a city van, drove us to Ironbound, showed us the gym, and asked, "Will this work?"

At this point it was put up or shut up. I told OB we would take it!

Due to my boxing experience at the Academy, and the positive impact it had on my life in the aftermath of my mom's stroke, I was adamant about running a free program. I knew I'd need to raise funds to cover the cost of operations and outfitting the gym, so I decided to start a nonprofit.

I joined forces with Gary Bloore, a retired business executive I met at St. Benedict's. Gary was teaching personal branding at the school and had an affinity for boxing. Once he heard I was coaching boxing at the school, he came and introduced himself and even offered to take some photos of me training the kids. At the time, Gary was in the early stages of running an organization called IRONBOUND USA, and since the free gym would be in the Ironbound section of Newark, I approached him about partnering together to bring the gym to life under one unified IRONBOUND umbrella.

He agreed. We partnered up and agreed to launch IRON-BOUND Boxing Academy.

We still needed funding. One of the caveats for receiving the free space from the city of Newark was that IRON-BOUND would be responsible for covering all costs associated with outfitting the gym.

After posting on my personal Facebook page about the new gym, mobilizing my personal network and communities, we quickly raised $10,000 to cover outfitting of the gym. Donations included $5,000 and a boxing ring from the NYPD Boxing Team, courtesy of retired NYPD police officer and amateur boxing enthusiast, Pat Russo, who runs multiple free boxing gyms in New York City under his organization, Cops & Kids. We also received support from multiple veteran-owned businesses, including SOF-LETE, a fitness company that specializes in programming, supplements, and apparel for special operations forces around the world.

Nearly five months after receiving the space, Gary, Keith, and I officially launched the IRONBOUND Boxing Academy in February of 2017.

"IRON" MIKE
Over the next year, I threw myself into learning anything and everything I could about running a successful

nonprofit, including how to raise necessary funds to keep the program growing. I enrolled in Introduction to Nonprofit Management as part of my graduate program in American Studies at Rutgers University-Newark.

During the summer of 2017, I attended an entrepreneur program at Stanford University for post-9/11 veterans called Stanford Ignite, a four-week in-person accelerator program that teaches veterans how to launch successful ventures. Stanford Ignite was the first formal entrepreneur training I received, and it was the first time I began to seriously look at myself as an entrepreneur, although not confidently.

Stanford Ignite reconnected me with the veteran community, which I had initially planned to distance myself from after leaving the military. I never felt like I could be myself in the military.

As a Black infantry officer, I often found myself as one of one. It was hard enough being a Marine officer, let alone a Black one. I felt immense pressure to excel because I knew that to many, I represented a whole race. The Marine Corps has an abysmal rate of success for Black infantry officers, many of whom never make it out of the infamous Infantry Officer Course, a three-month rigorous course which prepares Marine officers to become rifle platoon commanders. Black officers are often ranked lower than their peers, and there's an unofficial belief amongst Black service members that of all the services, the Marine Corps is the most racist, especially when it comes to its treatment of Black officers.

I experienced racism in the Marines.

During a training brief, in front of a classroom of my peers, a superior officer accused me of using slang and reminded me I'm "not in the ghetto" and that I "wasn't conducting a drive by." Even writing about it now makes my blood boil. Experiencing such open and blatant racism throughout my career, and the shame and guilt I felt after being relieved of combat, forced me to want to separate myself as much as possible from the Marines and the veteran community after I left active duty.

However, once Stanford Ignite introduced me to the veteran entrepreneur ecosystem, I regained a sense of connection and camaraderie. I discovered I actually enjoyed being around veterans pursuing entrepreneurial ambitions. I wanted to maintain the connection with them once the program ended. I did that and had the opportunity to create additional similar connections.

At the end of Stanford Ignite, I had the opportunity to get involved with Bunker Labs, a national network of veterans and military spouse entrepreneurs dedicated to helping veterans start and grow businesses. One of my peers during the program led the San Francisco chapter of Bunker Labs and went on to connect me with the New York City chapter.

Between Stanford Ignite and Bunker Labs, I found my tribe and the foundation on which IRONBOUND would stand and grow.

Once the broader veteran community found out I was running a free boxing gym for youth in Newark, they quickly mobilized around my efforts, donating to support the cause and amplifying our efforts with public relations opportunities.

Before I knew it, I was in the press promoting IRON-BOUND Boxing on national television and in magazines. Veterans from all over the country and all over the world reached out to me, expressing how much they believed in what my team and I were doing and how they wanted to help.

Through Bunker Labs, I had an opportunity to enroll in multiple education programs, including their recently launched Veterans in Residence (VIR), done in collaboration with WeWork, to provide veteran entrepreneurs and family members access to free coworking space and programming all across the country. The opportunity to be a member of the VIR lead to more press opportunities and more connections.

Network and community is everything. You can't succeed without it. I'll tell you more about that in Chapters 16 through 19.

A year after launching the IRONBOUND Boxing Academy, I found myself pulled more and more into the veteran entrepreneurial community and the feeling that I should focus on IRONBOUND Boxing full-time. At that time, our organization had less than $5,000 in the bank account, but I believed I could get us to the next level if I had the freedom and flexibility to do so. However, I would have to give all my time and attention to the program and nothing else, and before I could make the entrepreneurial leap to go full-time, I needed to find a way to cover my living expenses.

After I'd returned from Stanford in the summer of 2017, I enrolled in a course on social entrepreneurship at Rutgers Business School. The course introduced me to the concept of social enterprises, which are businesses with a social competence, whether that means having a nonprofit arm or contributing to society in a positive way strictly through their for-profit structure. Brands like Warby Parker, Toms Shoes, and others were examples of businesses doing good while doing well.

With that seed planted, over the next year I consumed countless podcasts, books, and articles in my attempt to develop a business model that would allow me to do good while doing well. Eventually, I came up with the idea to teach boxing to companies in the NYC metro area. I would be able to cover my initial personal expenses from the profits, and this for-profit side of IRONBOUND could allow me to hire kids from the gym, creating a professional growth path for them from IRONBOUND boxing trainees to corporate boxing trainers.

After giving myself a couple of pep talks, I stepped down from my role at St. Benedict's in the summer of 2018 to stand up a for-profit arm of IRONBOUND Boxing, focused on corporate wellness.

To fund the initial start-up cost, including my compensation, I liquidated my savings and leaped.

From the summer 2018 to summer 2020, I went through the entrepreneurial ringer. I ran myself ragged, attempting to bring my vision to life; coaching boxing during the day in NYC at companies like Next Jump, Spotify, and Etsy, all while coaching boxing in the evening at the IRONBOUND Boxing Academy in Newark.

During this time, I participated and won multiple pitch competitions, including a $25,000 grant from the Street Shares Foundation, allowing me to keep the IRONBOUND dream alive. Life was hard, but I was living it on my own terms. And I managed to build a somewhat stable living for myself up until the pandemic hit in March 2020. Like a lot of business owners, I was forced to start over from scratch.

With the lockdown and social distancing requirements, there was no longer a market for in-person boxing. The city of Newark forced us to close the IRONBOUND Boxing Academy, and my in-person clients no longer had a need for our on-site services. With the Academy closed, no clients, and zero revenue, I wasn't just on the rope, I was down hard on the canvas.

My Marine Corps training kicked in. I had to reassess my situation and improvise, adapt, and overcome, quickly.

Although our gym was closed, this didn't mean IRONBOUND Boxing couldn't still make an impact. Our goal all along had been to build champions in and out of the ring, and with Newark's local economy devastated by the pandemic, I had an idea for a new program called THRIVE.

My veteran entrepreneurial journey, specifically the exposure to training programs and pitch competitions, led me to want to start one for the kids in Newark under the IRONBOUND Boxing umbrella. With approval from our board of directors, which I stood up fall 2019, we launched THRIVE, a small business bootcamp intended to teach Newark teens the basics of launching a small business and to offer the opportunity for them to receive a microgrant between $500 and $2,000.

We kicked off the program in June 2020, training our first cohort of kids. Simultaneously, my partner Keith Colon began running social distancing workouts at Branch Brook Park to keep the kids training and active despite the IRONBOUND Boxing Academy's pandemic closure.

Although things were challenging, we were in a good place, thanks again to the veteran community who relentlessly came out to support us. Once word spread about THRIVE, we started receiving more and more donations, especially in the aftermath of the death of George Floyd and the racial unrest that summer. Due to the brand credibility I had built over the years with IRONBOUND Boxing, when George Floyd's death amplified the economic disparity in Black and Brown communities, and when it came time to support causes that mattered, many veterans looked toward IRONBOUND Boxing as their vehicle for promoting and supporting change.

While continuing to serve the community's youth through THRIVE, I also managed to spin up a new business model for our for-profit arm, leveraging technology to teach boxing remotely, albeit it I wasn't the biggest fan. For months I taught virtual boxing classes via Zoom while running THRIVE.

I knew virtual boxing classes weren't sustainable for me in the long term because I didn't enjoy it. Also, I accepted the reality that competitors like Peloton and Fight Camp 360 had way more technology support and capital than I did to dominate that market.

I began looking for an exit out of corporate boxing.

In February 2020, I launched my first podcast, *Confessions of a Native Son*, to share Black veterans' perspectives on race, culture, and business. I started the podcast to share my experiences dealing with racism in the military and America at large. I was frustrated by the lack of Black representation in the mainstream media, especially the perspectives of Black veterans.

I didn't want Americans to assume the bro-vet culture found on conservative news outlets, often standing against movements such as Black Lives Matter, not to be confused with the organization, represented me. *Confessions of a Native Son* presented me with an opportunity to own my narrative and share it with others.

I successfully launched the show and recorded episodes when I wasn't teaching virtual boxing classes or running

THRIVE. I recognized how much I enjoyed the process for myself, I was good at it, and I could help others do the same. I started exploring the idea of producing podcasts.

I took the idea to market and launched IRONBOUND Media, a podcast production company, in June of 2020.

I spread word of the launch to my network, and before I knew it I had my first paying client. Within a few months, I was earning enough revenue to safely exit from teaching virtual boxing classes and focus on IRON-BOUND Media full-time. On the outside, the transition from boxing to podcasting probably looks a little unusual, but the reality is that over the last three years promoting IRONBOUND Boxing, I managed to refine my gift of gab. My time on national media outlets and my public speaking opportunities translated well into the podcasting space.

Additionally, all the lessons I learned over the years running IRONBOUND Boxing quickly came together once I launched IRONBOUND Media, allowing me to achieve success relatively quickly. Within a year, I managed to grow IRONBOUND Media into six figures, producing podcasts for veteran-owned businesses and organizations. Concurrently, the IRONBOUND Boxing Academy eventually reopened after more than a year and half.

Today, both IRONBOUND Boxing and IRONBOUND Media are alive and thriving, although we still have so much to accomplish.

In addition to managing the day-to-day of both entities, I'm working on raising $1.5 million to bring our amateur boxing program and entrepreneur programs, which we run virtually, all under one roof. The vision is to build the first ever IRONBOUND Courage Academy, a boxing gym and small business incubator located in the heart of downtown Newark. You can think of it as a twenty-first century Boys and Girls Club.

In everything I do, there's an underlying thread to "lift as I climb," leveraging entrepreneurship to support the Black community in some way, whether through boxing or entrepreneurial endeavors.

As I look toward the future, not only to build IRON-BOUND Boxing and IRONBOUND Media into sustainable enterprises, I plan to invest in other founders of color, whether they create handcrafted goods they sell at local pop-ups in their communities or are early-stage start-up founders. I want to invest in entrepreneurs while teaching them everything I've learned through books, podcasts, and newsletters.

This book represents the first step.

HOW THIS APPLIES TO YOU:
- Where you start isn't where you're going to finish.
- Look for ways to leverage your own experiences to help someone else.
- You can't be afraid to take risks. Sometimes, you have to act on faith.

- Don't be afraid to use all things you've learned, whether you think they're helpful or not.

ADDITIONAL RESOURCES:

READ
- *The Alchemist* by Paul Coelho
- *The Alter Ego Effect: The Power of Secret Identities to Transform Your Life* by Todd Herman

LISTEN
- *Confessions of a Native Son*: "The Life of Times of a Black Marine Corps Infantry Officer"
- *Confessions of a Native Son*: "To Boxing with Love"

2

THE ROAD AHEAD

"If you can't fly then run, if you can't run then walk, if you can't walk then crawl, but whatever you do you have to keep moving forward."

—MARTIN LUTHER KING, JR.

Whether you want to admit it or not, we both know you're making it up as you go, especially in the early days.

What I have for you is a way forward.

Business ideas are a dime a dozen. The Small Business Administration estimates more than 600,000 new businesses are started each year, not including those unregistered.

Your challenge is knowing which ideas to act upon and how to bring them to life. You don't need an advanced business degree. It does help if you at least know the road ahead and how to navigate it.

DO NOT BE LIKE ME

I learned a lot of things the hard way. When I left my full-time job at St. Benedict's Prep, I didn't validate IRONBOUND Boxing's for-profit business model before I went all-in. I didn't know the first thing about sales and the importance of driving revenue during the validation phase. I assumed things would magically work out. Although it did work out, it wasn't magically, and my assumption at the time cost me my savings.

Although I gained some success with IRONBOUND Boxing to build upon, I reached that point through sheer will and determination, not business acumen. I went off my gut and applied the same strategy to our corporate wellness arm.

I envisioned working with companies like Google, Facebook, and Uber, running their employees through weekly boxing classes to improve their morale and overall employee wellness. Everyone I spoke to about my idea told me it sounded like a great business idea, so I took their word for it and launched the business.

The first few months were brutal.

I had no clients and quickly burned through cash, forcing me to liquidate all of my savings. I thought to myself, *What the hell am I doing? Have I made the right choice?* I remember thinking this as I laid on my couch, staring at the ceiling.

Thankfully, I received a lifeline from WeWork. They hired me for a part-time consulting gig to support the Veterans in Residence Program with Bunker Labs. This allowed me to earn some income so I could continue working on the business.

The WeWork gig gave me a cushion to build a boxing client base without stressing whether or not I would be able to pay my bills. During this time, I also connected with a channel partner named Exubrancy, one of the largest and most successful wellness companies in the NYC metro area.

Through an introduction via Bunker Labs, I met Liz Wilkes, Exubrancy's founder, who became my advisor and contracted me to teach boxing to their clientele. Over the span of a year, I went from earning approximately $500 a month in top line revenue to approximately $7,500 a month at the height of my corporate boxing business. After partnering with Exubrancy and having grown my own client base, I transitioned from consulting to focusing on boxing full-time.

Once the pandemic hit, on-site boxing classes were no longer an option, so I decided to shut down the business.

Looking back, I realize I set myself up for failure from the very beginning by not having a framework to validate my business model and a method to determine whether or not I was on the right track. Thankfully, I shifted into podcasting and met fellow entrepreneur and business designer, Michelle Warner.

She introduced me to a framework that helps founders successfully navigate the entrepreneurial journey.

THE FIVE STAGES OF SMALL BUSINESS GROWTH

"The Five Stages of Small Business Growth" is an article written by Neil C. Churchill and Virgina L. Lewis, published in the *Harvard Business Review* in 1983. In the article, Neil and Virginia discussed a business framework that breaks the entrepreneurial journey into the following five stages:

1. Existence
2. Survival
3. Success
4. Take-off
5. Maturity

Although the article is geared toward small businesses, the principals apply across the board, from nonprofits to venture backed-technology start-ups.

Start-up studios, organizations that repeatedly build businesses out of market-tested disruptive ideas while leveraging its pooled resources, utilize a similar framework to validate ideas and then spin them off for funding. Studios such as Pioneer Square Labs, based in Seattle, have spun out over twenty-five companies in the last five years, utilizing a similar framework to the one above.

In meeting Michelle, I learned about the original five stage framework. She also introduced me to the framework she'd used for herself to make the original more digestible for early stage founders.

Michelle's Five Stages:
1. Validate
2. Sales
3. Foundation
4. Expand
5. Multiply

Stage 1: Validate

Validation starts by verifying you have a product or service someone is willing to pay for. While it may sound redundant, you'd be surprised how many people skip this step. The only way to validate your business model is to charge someone for your products and services, then receive payment. Everything else is a vanity metric in my opinion.

For some entrepreneurs, this may not be feasible, especially for those building tech products that require a large upfront investment. However, there are ways around this, such as launching a pre-sale campaign or tracking sign-ups. It's imperative you charge right away, because advice from friends and family can be a false positive, i.e., incorrect data. Avoid making decisions based on pure assumptions. Make your assumptions, then verify with paying customers. If someone believes you have a good idea, charge them on the spot and see if they'd be willing to put their money where their mouth is.

Stage 2: Sales

Once you get a few beta customers and realize you have something people are willing to pay for, the next step is to focus on generating monthly recurring revenue (MRR). Most BVEs need to reach profitability as soon as possible, unless you're a venture-backed tech start-up with millions of dollars in the bank. You need to maintain healthy cash flow at all times. Either way, it can't hurt to demonstrate traffic with paying customers, as it shows the viability of your business model.

That's why stage two is about good ol' fashion sales. At times it can feel like hand-to-hand combat, especially going from one to ten customers, then ten to one-hundred, because it feels like you're going to war each and every day. You're going to be tempted by other distractions, such as crafting the next social media post. But at the end of the day, sales drives revenue, and if you're a bootstrapped founder or small business owner, oftentimes the responsibility for sales falls on you. To be honest, if you're an early stage founder period, it's more than likely you're responsible for sales.

The same goes for nonprofits. Sales and fundraising go hand in hand. In order to run your program effectively and provide the impact you want, you'll need funding support, whether it's five thousand dollars or five million. Don't neglect it.

The goal for the sales stage is to reach a point where you can predict your monthly recurring revenue three to six months in advance, which will allow you to be more strategic with how you run your business, including bringing on more staff or investing in marketing assets, without the risks of going bankrupt. Once you do, you can focus on building out your business foundations.

Stage 3: Foundation

The next stage in your business is to build your foundation. This includes thinking through how you scale up by identifying the key personnel and capabilities you need and who will fill those slots. In my case, my first hire was an administrative assistant to help me run the nonprofit during the pandemic.

At a certain point, no matter how amazing you think you are, you can't do everything alone. As you start building out your team, identify the core functions you need filled, i.e., jobs that need to be done, such as creating marketing assets for your business, reaching out to prospects, and so on. Identify your key role in your process, which more than likely is driving sales, and start to work on outsourcing everything else so you can focus on driving revenue.

Don't feel pressured to rush through stage three. Take as much time as you need and build your "A Team" before moving on to expansion.

Stage 4: Expand

Stage four is about scaling up and expanding. If you have a physical location, maybe this means doubling, or even tripling, your footprint. Before you consider expanding, make sure you have a solid foundation, because things will only get more complicated.

Stage 5: Multiply

This is when you step it up and go for scale. For a small business, multiply could mean expanding into some sort of franchise model or just scaling across the country. The choice is yours, just make sure you set conditions. Multiplying might mean raising venture capital, taking out a bank loan, or giving up part ownership if it means having the necessary capital to multiply accordingly.

Multiplying increases the complexity of your venture, and you want to ensure you don't delude quality for the sake of scale. We all know our favorite restaurants who never quite taste the same as the first location. If scaling up isn't done right, the things that make the original venture magical get lost in translation.

Of all the business tools and frameworks I've come across, the Five Stages are the best conceptual framework for understanding how-to successfully navigate the entrepreneurial journey. Not only do I preach it to every entrepreneur I come across, it's also a core component of our entrepreneurial curriculum at THRIVE.

Let me walk you through how the Black- and veteran-owned company, Dope Coffee, successfully used the Five Stages.

1. Validate
2. Sales
3. Foundation
4. Expand
5. Multiply

DOPE COFFEE COMPANY

Mike Loyd, Marine Corps veteran, and his wife, Michelle, came up with the idea for an e-commerce coffee brand called Dope Coffee in Summer 2019. After years of experience running a brick and mortar coffee kiosk called Solar Cafe in Hempstead, North Carolina, Mike and Michelle felt confident in their ability to transition into e-commerce.

They'd also become increasingly frustrated by the lack of representation of Black culture in the modern coffee industry, so they decided to address the problem head on, launching a coffee brand infused with hip hop, community, and Black culture.

As a Marine combat engineering officer originally from Winston-Salem, North Carolina, Mike got his passion for coffee from his mother, and it grew during his years in the military, particularly while on deployment in Afghanistan.

One day while walking around Camp Leatherneck, the Marine Corps' forward operating base in Afghanistan, Mike came across a coffee kiosk made out of plywood. And even though it was made out of plywood, it was a successful shop. Mike was confident he could replicate the model, though not literally out of plywood, back in the states.

After he returned from deployment and relocated his family from San Diego to North Carolina, Mike and Michelle launched Solar Cafe, a drive-through coffee kiosk similar to the one in Afghanistan.

Solar Cafe validated their initial business model and what they later developed into Dope Coffee. Customers were interested in their coffee and in their brand in a market that's already saturated. After running Solar Cafe for a year, and generating upward of $100,000 and more in revenue, they hired staff and expanded their footprint in Hempstead. The couple went on to run Solar Cafe for four years, operating multiple locations, until a hurricane hit their local community, destroyed their kiosks, and forced Mike and Michelle to rethink their original business model.

After a few months, the couple decided to pivot into e-commerce.

VALIDATE

In an effort to rebuild and recover from their loss, the couple moved their family to Decatur, Georgia, and rebranded Solar Cafe as Dope Coffee.

Mike, also a rapper with a deep passion for Black culture, envisioned building a company that promotes Black culture, including music and art, as well as economic empowerment. His vision included building a business model where Black people integrated into every aspect of the coffee industry, from farmer to consumer. Just like before, Mike knew he and his team had to be strategic and revisit the five stages of small business growth to pull their vision off for Dope Coffee.

They started doing local coffee pop-ups around town and at universities to ensure there was a demand for Dope Coffee in the Atlanta area and it's infusion of Black culture. This also gave them the opportunity to collect emails in preparation for driving traffic to their website. After earning thousands of dollars and seeing the engagement they received on social media, the team knew they had a valid business idea.

They could confidently move on to the next stage.

SALES

The next step was to launch the website. They planned for the website to drive the bulk of their sales effort, transitioning from validation into the sales stage. As they transitioned to the next stage they knew it would be a slow burn to get traffic to the site to generate enough revenue for the business to be profitable.

They set up an aggressive social media strategy, worked with IRONBOUND Media to create the podcast *Confessions of a Native Son*, and tapped into their veteran network, participating in programs with Bunker Labs and other organizations in their local area.

After driving traffic to their website for over a year, via pop-ups and word of mouth, Mike and his team began generating predictable revenue between $5,000 to $10,000 a month. This revenue allowed them to grow their team and transition into the foundation stage.

FOUNDATION

As revenue continued to roll in and systems started breaking, Mike and Michelle knew they had built a rock solid foundation, including their team and distribution process. The year prior, Mike brought on his cousin, Stacey Loyd, to assume the role of chief marketing officer (CMO) so he could remove marketing from his plate and focus on fundraising and driving business development while Michelle focused on product.

They team also hired a digital marketing assistant to run social media and fulfillment staff to assist with the online orders.

They began streamlining their systems and processes, building out their back office in Google Docs to turn Dope Coffee into a well-oiled machine.

With their sales in place and their foundation set, they knew they were ready to expand.

EXPAND

To keep up with demand and position themselves for long-term sustainable growth, Mike and Michelle realized they needed capital. After multiple unsuccessful attempts to raise venture capital, they turned to the people and executed multiple crowdfunding campaigns, each raising upwards of $100,000.

With the funding, they were able to expand Dope Coffee's operations from the Atlanta area to Mike's hometown, Winston Salem. And they also began to offer new products, including K-cup pods and more.

MULTIPLY

The team is still maturing and growing. And their multiply stage is on the horizon.

If you want to be "dope" and support them along the way, you can learn more by visiting their website www.RealDope. Coffee

HOW THIS APPLIES TO YOU:

- Understand how to create and then validate a business model before launching.
- Learn and understand the five stages of small business growth and how it applies to your business and business ideas.
- Know what stage your business is in.
- Set a time frame for when you want to transition to the next stage.
- Know what criteria you need to reach to transition to the next stage.

ADDITIONAL RESOURCES:

READ

- "The Five Stages of Small Business Growth" by Neil C. Churchill and Virginia L. Lewis
- "Understand Your Business Stage" by Michelle Warner
- *The Start-Up J Curve: The Six Steps to Entrepreneurial Success* by Howard Love

- *The Transition* podcasts: "The 5 Stages of Small Business Growth with Michelle Warner, Business Strategist & Designer"

3

COMING UP WITH YOUR IDEA

"I believe in destiny. But I also believe that you can't just sit back and let destiny happen. A lot of times, an opportunity might fall into your lap, but you have to be ready for that opportunity. You can't sit there waiting on it. A lot of times you are going to have to get out there and make it happen."

—SPIKE LEE

If you're like me, you've probably come up with multiple business ideas over the years, some good and some bad.

Whether that's dreaming about starting a food truck, opening your own fitness studio, or building a technology product, we've all been there. What I've come to learn is the difference between those who bring their vision to life and the ones who constantly talk about it is that one group is willing to take action, while the other is not.

Don't let the latter be you.

You have to cultivate an idea and care for it like an indoor plant that always looks like it is struggling to survive. Like the plant, your idea might not thrive at first, but the more you nourish it over time, the more it will take on a life of its own. From there, the market will dictate its value, but you can increase your chances for success by knowing what to look for when evaluating your idea.

I suggest you start by coming up with a business idea that solves a particular problem for a specific group of people who are willing to donate or pay you money to solve it. Make sure your idea is something you're passionate about so that when times get rough, and they will, you'll be motivated to keep moving forward.

The best business ideas come from founders with a thorough understanding of the problem they're addressing and why they're the ones to solve it. In the age of non-fungible tokens (or NFTs), cryptocurrency, and new forms of emerging technology, it's easy to fall into the trap of pursuing a speculative business idea because it looks like a good opportunity instead of pursuing one where you already have some advantage.

A great place to start is by asking yourself, Why are you the one to solve this particular problem?

As an example, we'll take a look at UpSkill VR.

UPSKILL VR

Carla Bond, a Navy veteran, came up with the idea of using virtual reality to train students and professionals, including first-responders, nurses, teachers, and military units.

While on active duty, Carla served as a Naval police officer and Fleet Marine Force hospital corpsman. She also served as an emergency management specialist for the Department of Health and Human Services and as an instructor trainer in emergency response. She underwent rigorous training and certifications for all of her positions. After a while, the training and certification process seemed archaic and inconvenient in an increasing digital world where online certifications and on-demand training were now the norm.

Due to the hands-on nature of the job, CPR training had yet to catch up to the digital world, so Carla began seeking solutions.

One day, while searching on online, Carla came across a video of elementary kids in virtual reality headsets. The video piqued her interest.

As a mother of three girls and one boy, Carla found the idea fascinating. Her curiosity with virtual reality began as a child.

During an episode of *The Transition Podcast*, Carla told me:

I was watching a video online one day, and these kindergartners traveled to DC in virtual reality. I reached out to the video creator, inquiring if the kids were tested on their trip.

The video's creator responded to Carla's email that not only were the kids tested, but they also showed a 40 percent increase in performance compared to a control group of kids who only read about DC in a textbook.

I figured if a five-year-old could learn from virtual reality, why not adults?

As an instructor trainer, Carla couldn't get over the outdated way these professionals received emergency response training like CPR, which occurred every two years and was often identical to the exact same training from the previous years. *There has to be a better way,* she thought to herself.

I remember running a call [as an EMT] to an unresponsive child. When we got to the scene, the little boy was still wedged between the toilet and the tub, and he was in cardiac arrest. En route to the hospital, his mother told me she has been in the medical field for over twenty years. But when we got to the scene, she was so emotionally distraught, scared, and crying that she didn't even start CPR on him. She'd sat through at least ten CPR trainings in her career, but when the manikin became her son, all bets were off. Her training went out the window. That was the straw that broke the camel's back for me. I knew the way I was training people had to change. I had to get them ready for the real world, not just pass a test and get a card.

She tried different methods to make the training more realistic. She knew from her years of experience as an EMT that nothing beats real-world training. Learning those life saving skills not only requires physical repetition but emotional memorization as well.

She realized she could bring the real-world into the classroom using virtual reality (VR).

Not only would VR allow for more realistic training scenarios, such as the ability to conduct CPR while at the scene of an actual wreck, the sensors and feedback would also allow them to refine their craft using technology. A virtual headset would transform training that was usually held in an empty classroom into a scene where a victim in a work environment was in need of CPR.

I wanted to bring the real-world experience into the classroom.

From her idea, Carla founded UpSkill VR.

Carla taught herself the basics of developing VR, leveraging YouTube, books, online courses, and anything she could get her hands on. She liquidated all of her savings so she could hire individual software developers to help create the initial training scenarios.

From there, she recruited a chief technology officer (CTO) to help with product development. Carla developed the training scenarios, and her CTO oversaw the developers who built the software.

UpSkill VR's initial business model was originally through licensing agreements with the CPR certification bodies.

She found that route extremely difficult in the early stages, so she had to pivot. They transitioned UpSkill VR into a software-as-a-service platform for individuals to sign up and stay up to date with all their training requirements on-demand using VR.

Carla cleared a direct path to those who needed training.

Since launching UpSkill VR, Carla was featured as a Forbes Next 1000. The Next 1000 showcases ambitious founders in every region of the country with infinite drive and hustle that are game-changers in their industries. She's also a recipient of cash awards from companies such as Google and grants from WeWork and the Small Business Administration (SBA).

Carla came up with and took action on her idea, an idea that checked all the boxes.

- Solves a problem for a specific group of people
- The group of people are willing to donate or pay money to solve the problem
- It is an idea she is passionate about
- It is a business idea where she already has an advantage

This checklist is a great starting point for you.

HOW THIS APPLIES TO YOU:
- Identify a problem you're passionate about solving and think creatively about solutions to solve it.

- Look for ideas within your immediate network, from your day to day observations, going to work, spending time with friends, or walking around your local community.
- Start nourishing your idea by getting it on paper and mapping what you hope to accomplish in the long term.

ADDITIONAL RESOURCES:

READ
- *The Common Path to Uncommon Success: A Roadmap to Financial Freedom and Fulfillment* by John Lee Dumas
- *Category Pirates Newsletter:* "Living Your Category POV: Why Founder/CEO-Problem Fit Defines Whether You Are a Missionary or a Mercenary"

LISTEN
- Seth Godin's "Start-up School" podcast
- MicroConf on Air: "Designing the Ideal Bootstrapped Business" by Jason Cohen, founder of WP Engine

4

THE SIMPLIFIED BUSINESS PLAN

"Every great dream begins with a dreamer. Always remember, you have within you the strength, the patience, and the passion to reach for the stars to change the world."

—HARRIET TUBMAN

A robust business plan with financial projections, salaries, and everything else has it's time and place; *however*, in the early days of launching a venture, it's unnecessary, especially in the validation stage.

In Chapter 1, I told you when I first launched IRON-BOUND Boxing I had zero business acumen. I meant that. I studied history at the Naval Academy and spent five years in the Marine Corps learning and teaching advanced infantry tactics to fellow Marines. However, I didn't let my lack of formal business education stop me from pursuing entrepreneurship. Instead, I spent my time reading and listening to everything business oriented I could get my hands on.

Through my self-education, personal experiences, and insight from thought leaders and mentors, I developed a simplified business plan I now use for all of my ventures and projects.

My simplified business plan is comprised of four components:

- A description of your idea
- The problem you're solving
- Why your business is the solution
- Your immediate next steps

When Gary and I came together to discuss the IRON-BOUND Boxing Academy in the fall of 2016, we used a less refined version of this framework. However, the simplified approach quickly proved useful and preferable to pages and pages of a business plan. We knew we wanted to open a badass boxing gym in Newark, and so we got to it.

We began with describing our idea and went from there.

OUR BIG IDEA

We wanted to open a badass boxing gym in Newark, a gym that got kids off the street and in the ring training and being around positive role models. From the very beginning, we established that the gym was meant to serve as a feeder program to educational programs we wanted to offer in the future, including classes on personal branding, financial literacy, entrepreneurship, and more.

Although we had grand ambitions, the immediate task was bringing the IRONBOUND Boxing Academy to life.

THE PROBLEM

We asked ourselves, and each other, the immediate question, "What problem can the IRONBOUND Boxing Academy, specifically, solve?"

At the time, nearly 30 percent of Newark's population lived below the poverty line. The majority of whom congregated in low-income areas, such as housing projects near the IRONBOUND Boxing Academy's location. We concluded that as a result, parents in these communities more than likely couldn't afford to pay for high quality recreation programs like what we were offering at the Academy.

With more than half of these families' income going to cover food and rent expenses alone, there's little to no financial flexibility for extracurricular activities.

WHY WE WERE THE SOLUTION

We identified the problem, so we had our solution—The IRONBOUND Boxing Academy needed to be a free amateur boxing gym for Newark's youth and young adults, with the intent to change lives through boxing.

The kids we wanted to serve were some of the most vulnerable to the streets. They needed a safe place where they could build a rapport with and learn from positive mentors. We didn't want the program to be your traditional after-school program, one they may have been to before that didn't click with them and their needs. The space needed to be a place where they could be themselves, have agency, and pursue something they were deeply passionate about, like boxing.

Fortunately, boxing gave us a certain level of street credibility and instant brand awareness that other after-school and nontraditional recreation programs didn't have. In 2016, amateur boxer and Newark native Shakur Stevenson put the city on the map with his performance in the Brazil Olympics. We were able to capitalize on that with the youth in the area, thanks to Shakur.

IMMEDIATE NEXT STEPS
We identified the problem, found the solution, and now were able to map out the next three to five steps. We identified what gets us going; what drives the momentum. The immediate actions needed to move forward are some of the most important aspects of a simplified business plan.

Over the years, I've lost count of the friends, family members, and fellow veterans who come to me with a great idea, but when it comes to nourishing it and bringing it to life, they're unable to connect the dots. Taking the time to map out even three next steps works wonders in keeping the dream alive.

In order to keep moving forward, our next steps were clear to us:

- Clean and prepare the gym for launch
- Launch a basic website
- Raise initial funding for gear and equipment

For the next five months, we spent our time executing the plan above. It wasn't sexy, but it was enough to get the momentum going.

I'm a big proponent of the philosophy "kaizen," a Japanese term meant to convey the idea of "consistent incremental improvement over time." Your plan doesn't have to be perfect right out the gate. You can always update it and look for areas where you can optimize.

When you catch the idea wave, you need to capitalize on it while you can.

ACTION VERSUS MOMENTUM

At this point, I want you to take action, and the easiest way to do so is by cranking open a Google document or pulling out some pen and paper and writing your idea down. If not, as author James Clear describes in his book, *Atomic Habits: An Easy and Proven Way to Build Good Habits and Break Bad Ones*, you risk being in motion versus taking action.

"When you're in motion, you're planning and strategizing and learning. Those are all good things, but they don't produce a result. Action, on the other hand, is the type of behavior that will deliver an outcome."

What separates veterans from non-veterans is our bias for action, so get started.

HOW THIS APPLIES TO YOU:
- Create a simplified one-page business plan on a piece of paper, Google document, or white board.
- Capture the core ideas of your venture and build a plan you can grow into; it doesn't have to be perfect.
- Share the plan with key stakeholders, including cofounders, initial donors, and anyone else involved in the process.
- Constantly refer back to the plan as you develop your venture.

ADDITIONAL RESOURCES:

READ
- "The Mistake Smart People Make: Being In Motion versus Taking Action," by James Clear, from his book, *Atomic Habits: An Easy and Proven Way to Build Good Habits and Break Bad Ones.*

LISTEN
- *The Peter Attia Drive Podcasts*: "James Clear: Building and Changing Habits"

5

FIND YOUR PERFECT CUSTOMER

"When people show you who they are, believe them the first time."

—MAYA ANGELOU

If you want a one-way ticket to the start-up grave-yard, chase the illusive product market fit, a market with a strong demand for what you're selling. Unfortunately, Silicon Valley is buried with would-be start-ups that ran out of cash trying to find it. Don't let that be you!

Don't believe me? Well, guess what? The numbers don't lie.

According to data from the Bureau of Labor Statistics, as reported by Fundera, "Approximately 20 percent of small businesses fail within the first year. By the end of the second year, 30 percent of businesses will have failed. By the end of the fifth year, about half will have failed. And by the end of the decade, only 30 percent of businesses will remain—a 70 percent failure rate."

A large percentage of the failure rate is due to no market need for the companies' products or services, second only to running out of cash.

In order to kill two birds with one stone, build your venture with the intent to serve one perfect customer. A customer who is willing to pay you a premium for your products or services, consistently makes warm referrals on your behalf, and makes you enjoy being an entrepreneur.

If you participate in an incubator or accelerator program, they'll encourage you to identify a total addressable market (TAM), such as health care or education, with a large market cap (example: $1 billion), and identify the percentage of the market you can go after. This results in BVEs believing if they can capture a small percentage of a billion dollar market, they'll be millionaires. Tada!

I don't recommend you take that approach.

Instead, I strongly encourage you to build a market around your perfect customer. They fill up your bank account and entrepreneurial spirit instead of draining them, and the sooner you learn how to identify them, the faster you can build a profitable and sustainable business.

To succeed as a BVE, focus on your perfect customer from *day one!*

TRAITS OF A PERFECT CUSTOMER

The most important trait of a perfect customer is that you enjoy working with them and they value you. How they engage with you and your team, and their willingness to financially compensate you for your services will demonstrate this to you.

If someone is paying you pennies on the dollars, or is never satisfied, or it feels risky doing business with them in the first place, they're not your perfect customer.

The following are traits and characteristics of your perfect customer:
- They have a problem your company is uniquely positioned to solve and are willing to spend money for you to solve it.
- They can afford what you are offering.
- You already have some form of trust and credibility established with them based on your affiliations, e.g. professional network, college alumni, etc.
- You share similar values.

Just as important as it is to identify who they are, it is equally important to be clear on who they are not. If a prospective customer constantly asks for free samples or consultations, which never result in an actual purchase, take that as a confirmation that's not what you want.

Avoid customers who:
- Drain you and your team.
- Challenges your pricing.
- Takes up to and beyond sixty to ninety days to pay you.

Regardless of your venture type, by adopting the lens of your perfect customer, you put yourself in the best possible position to succeed as an entrepreneur, bar none. Understanding your perfect customer will set the foundation for your company's marketing plan, which you'll build upon to drive revenue.

YOUR PATH TO IDENTIFYING YOUR PERFECT CUSTOMER

CAN YOU PROVIDE VALUE?

Start by asking yourself, "Who am I uniquely positioned to serve?" and "Where am I able to provide them the most value?"

For example:

Let's say you have an idea for a business that helps low-income students get into their colleges of choice by helping them ace the ACTs and SATs.

First, you need to identify what sets you apart, i.e., getting students into Ivy League colleges or helping them get scores that result in full tuition.

Since your goal is to serve low-income students, let's assume it's unlikely their parents can afford to pay a premium price point for your services. Rather than focusing your market efforts to attract parents, it would make more sense to target the universities, foundations, and other key stakeholders who need help preparing low-income students for standardized tests.

The ability to help low-income students ace standardized tests is a strong value proposition for entities looking to fund them. If the students are also athletes and don't have time or transportation to commute to tutoring sessions, and need someone to work with them at home or over Zoom, you can set your company apart by offering in-person and virtual tutoring.

This solves an immediate need for both the young stakeholder and the entities supporting them.

IDENTIFY THE ECONOMIC BUYER

Once you identify where you can provide the most value, the next step is to determine your price points and verify your perfect customer can afford them.

It doesn't make sense to offer premium consulting services or products to customers who can't afford to pay. You need to determine the income or budget of your perfect customer—and also whether or not they have a history of spending money in a market similar to yours.

In the words of Alan Weiss, contrarian consultant, the goal is to do business with the economic buyer, e.g. the person who can cut the check.

According to Weiss, "The economic buyer is the person who can write a check in return for your value contribution. He or she is the *only* buyer to be concerned about. Contrary to a great deal of poor advice, the economic buyer is virtually never in human resources, training, meeting planning, or related support areas."

Think back to your time in the military, where actuals talked to actuals, commander to commander. Rank didn't matter as much as the position of authority and responsibility you held.

In our example above, we identified the parents more than likely are not in the position to be the perfect customer; however, there are other entities who can cut the check who are interested and invested in low-income students getting into their university of choice.

With this example in mind, the next step is to identify heads of admissions at universities, executive directors of funding sources, and potentially government officials whose responsibility is to help increase the number of low-income students getting into colleges. From there you'd zero in even more. You'd want to look at those who have a track record of spending money on similar programs. That could include funding grants for youth development, after-school tutoring programs, and other programs bridging the gap between high school and secondary school.

If you were to charge twenty to fifty thousand dollars for a six-month engagement, it's safe to assume the organizations have an operating budget upward of at least two hundred to five hundred thousand dollars a year at the very least, if not more.

In this part of the process, it comes down to:
- Who can pay you? (Cut the check.)
- Can they afford you? (Do they have the funding or budget?)

The same process applies for product-based businesses.

For example:
If you want to sell high-end apparel, start looking for customers who already spend as much, if not more, on similar clothing items. They are the economic buyer in this situation, and they have a track record proving they can afford you.

WHERE TO START LOOKING

You don't have to look far when trying to find your perfect customer. Your perfect customer is all around you, in communities and organizations you are already a part of, where people already know, like, and trust you.

Think about the following people:
- College classmates
- Members of neighborhood associations
- Previous coworkers
- Fellow church members
- Friends and family

In your business's early days, you cannot afford the time and the monetary resources trying to sell to people you have no formal or informal relationship with. Cold outreach is a waste of time and money in the beginning. When you focus within your current communities you will establish your brand credibility and create a strong client list well before you could ever hope to with cold outreach.

The goal is to work smarter, not harder.

Continuing with the tutoring example above, I'd start with activating alumni or professional networks to determine if anyone works at the funding sources I'm targeting. And then, I'd determine how to most effectively engage with them, whether that means grabbing coffee, or jumping on a call, or simply connecting via email.

The key is to get the conversation going.

I've seen many entrepreneurs rush success and chase after the big clients, but sometimes you have to start with what you know and find trustworthy evangelists of your products or services within your network.

When I launched IRONBOUND Boxing, my network and community provided the majority of the donations. Colleagues, family and friends, fellow veterans, and those within their extended networks were happy to support my venture in any way they could. I didn't really need to do more than tell them what I was doing, because they knew me, they trusted me, and they knew I'd do exactly what I set out to do.

HOW I FOUND THE PERFECT CUSTOMER

For the first few years of my entrepreneurial journey, I didn't know the first thing about finding my perfect customer. Thankfully, I connected with Bill Watkins, a business coach who set me on the right path.

Bill is the founder and CEO of The Lions Pride (TLP), a professional training and coaching company for badass mission-driven founders. I joined their program in 2019 to help me grow IRONBOUND Boxing and to improve my overall business acumen.

The IRONBOUND Boxing Academy was still closed in December 2020 due to the pandemic and I was only a few months into IRONBOUND Media, my new venture, when Bill asked me an important question.

During our quarterly planning session with TLP members Bill asked me, "Mike, who is your perfect customer for IRONBOUND Media?"

I responded, "My perfect customer is a veteran small business owner or nonprofit executive who wants to start a podcast and share his or her lessons on entrepreneurship and leadership."

Before I could finish my sentence, BJ Kreamer, another TLP cohort member, Army veteran, and West Point graduate who runs a construction management firm called MCFA, took himself off mute and shouted, "That's me! When can we meet?"

I asked BJ for his email to schedule an initial call. BJ and I met three days later, and he became an IRONBOUND Media client. From that moment forward, I've been a true believer in finding your perfect customer and preach it every chance I get!

I wish I could say it was always this easy. Unfortunately, it's not. However, when you have a tight understanding of your perfect customer and where to find them, it's on you to earn their trust and close the deal. I didn't know at the time that my perfect customer would be on a Zoom call with me, but because I could describe them in specific detail, I got one's attention.

Visit BlackVeteranEntrepreneurs.com/PerfectCustomer to download your Identify Your Perfect Customer worksheet.

HOW THIS APPLIES TO YOU:
- Focus on your perfect customer for day one.
- Identify your not so perfect customer as well.
- Look for customers who already have a reason to know, like, and trust you.
- Ensure they can afford to pay you what you're worth.
- Only work with clients and customers you enjoy doing business with.

ADDITIONAL RESOURCES:

READ
- *Superconsumers: A Simple, Speedy, and Sustainable Path to Superior Growth* by Eddie Yoon
- *Superfans: The Easy Way to Stand Out, Grow Your Tribe, and Build a Successful Business* by Pat Flynn

LISTEN

- Dog Whistle Branding: "Screw Product Market Fit, Go Find your Perfect Customer"
- Dog Whistle Branding: "Scaling Your Perfect Customer by Identifying Your Dream One-Hundred with Eric Bakey, Founder of Combat Imagineer"

6

BUILD YOUR BRAND

"The thing about branding is it isn't etched in stone. A brand is a mark or an image or a perception we stamp on a product, a concept or an ideal, but it doesn't last forever. Like anything else, it needs to be nurtured and reinforced, or it will start to fade."

—DAYMOND JOHN, COFOUNDER OF FUBU

A BVEs worst enemy is a bad brand.

Bad brands are confusing, lack clarity of purpose, and show no differentiation from your competitors. A strong brand stands for something and serves a beacon of hope to your perfect customer. If you want to get their attention, then you have to be intentional about building your brand.

Building brands is my favorite part of being an entrepreneur. There's something magical about creating a brand out of thin air and making others give a damn about it.

I launched my first brand, Fighting Mojo, a fitness and lifestyle company, in the summer of 2012. At the time, I had no idea what the hell I was doing. However, I knew I wanted to create a brand that allowed me to express myself and my love for boxing. I started the brand during the last month of my deployment to Afghanistan. A time when I felt like I had lost my mojo and needed to get back (hence the name).

When I returned back to the states, I hit the ground running, hiring a graphic designer to make a logo. I built and launched a website and registered my first LLC. I didn't have a formal business model at the time, I just knew I wanted to share inspirational content and sell apparel on the internet. Within a few months, I printed my first run of T-shirts and shorts and began selling them out the trunk of my car to fellow officers in my battalion and classmates from the Naval Academy.

I was proud of what I was building because it was mine. Over the next few years, Fighting Mojo spread throughout my personal network as more and more friends began ordering apparel online and rocking T-shirts. I constantly got tagged on social media by friends in Fighting Mojo gear and would often get phone calls about how someone saw a Fighting Mojo T-shirt around town.

Outside of having something to be proud of, I didn't have a sustainable business model for Fighting Mojo. I was barely breaking even, and by the time I transitioned off of active duty in April 2015, the brand began to fizzle out.

Looking back, I don't think I would've done anything different, I was young and inexperienced at the time.

Fighting Mojo allowed me to get my feet wet and gave me a solid foundation to build upon to later launch IRON-BOUND Boxing.

Since then, I've learned a lot more about what it takes to build a successful brand in the age of the internet, where it appears everyone is competing for attention. Your brand needs to be the differentiating factor that sets you apart. Building a brand is more than a logo and a website. It's about positioning your company in a way that conveys to your perfect customer who you are and what you stand for and that you are for them.

When I launched Fighting Mojo, I did it to express myself, not to serve customers, which is why it wasn't successful long term. I didn't have a sense of purpose beyond myself to keep it going.

Branding isn't just about you, it's also about your customers and your team and how you're consistently earning and maintaining their trust and confidence.

At this point you've already identified your perfect customer in the previous chapter. Now it's time to build a brand to serve them.

At a minimum, you'll need the following:
- Core purpose
- Core values
- Bold beliefs
- Building your brand around your perfect customer
- The ability to connect the dots of all the above

There was a time in my life when I thought all of the above was corny and nothing but fluff, especially once I went full-time on my venture. The last thing I wanted to think about was core values when I needed to put money in the bank account. Now I know better. If you don't brand your company and establish who you are and what you stand for, you won't know and no one else will either.

START WITH THE CORE

All of us start our ventures for different reasons. Some of us want to escape the rat race of the nine to five life, and entrepreneurship represents an opportunity to do so while maintaining financial freedom. For others, we want to fund a project in our local community to make life better for the have-nots.

Whatever your reason, your branding is your vehicle to convey your purpose to the world.

Simon Sinek, author of *Start with Why*, sagely states, "There are only two ways to influence human behavior: you can manipulate it or you can inspire it. Very few people or companies can clearly articulate *why* they do *what* they do. By *why* I mean your purpose, cause or belief—*why* does your company exist? *Why* do you get out of bed every morning? And *why* should anyone care? People don't buy *what* you do, they buy *why* you do it."

I'm writing this book because I believe in the impact that BVEs can bring to our nation and our communities. Who knows what the future holds for the BVE platform I'm building, beginning with this book. But what I can tell you, the *why* will always be centered around educating and empowering BVEs to succeed.

Why do you want to launch your venture? What are you hoping to accomplish? What is the change you aim to bring to the world and your customers? These are questions only you and your team can answer–key word, *team!*

While it's important to understand your personal why, such as to create generational wealth for your family and loved ones, when it comes to your company's core purpose, it needs to be something that rallies your troops! As important as it may be for you to build generational wealth, I doubt that will motivate a vendor at the eleventh hour to jump out of bed in the middle of the night to email something to a client.

Your company's core purpose is bigger than you and needs to be inspirational.

At IRONBOUND Boxing our core purpose is to "build champions in and out of the ring." As an organization we aren't winning if all we do is set kids up for success as amateur or professional boxers. While it's great to see them win championships, we want them to have opportunities in life beyond boxing, such as attending college, going to trade school, or even starting their own business. This is what fuels us and why we exist.

Our core is what unites funders, volunteers, and anyone who supports the brand. It also empowers them to act on our behalf in our absence.

For example, one of our board members, Stephen Morris, approached the board of directors about starting a scholarship fund to enable our young athletes to attend college or trade schools. Right off the bat, everyone agreed this was a great idea because it was within our core purpose. Not only had he also managed to fund the scholarship right off the bat, now we have an additional program where we are able to offer support to our young stakeholders.

At IRONBOUND Media our core purpose is to "give our clients a brand and voice they can be proud of." To us, audio represents the future of publishing. For many of our clients, a podcast is their first real foray into sharing their thoughts and opinions with the world. Getting it right is important to them, so it's important to us. This includes everything from their cover art to the quality of their audio. If we upload bad audio or brand assets that disappoint our clients, we're failing to live up to our core.

Some companies don't care about their clients' churn rate once they receive payment. For us, it's about so much more. We are stewards within the veteran community, and we serve our clients through our services, which we take pride in.

While some management philosophies encourage you to develop a vision and mission statement, all that comes secondary in my book to your core purpose. Your core is the foundation your brand needs to build upon.

CORE VALUES

Your core values are the traits, behaviors, and characteristics of you and your team. While they can be aspirational in nature, more importantly they need to live up to who you are and how you operate as a company.

In the military, we adopted the core values of honor, courage, and commitment. While those may work for a large robust military organization, they don't capture the soul and the spirit of BVE ventures. Embrace the fact that you are building something from scratch and infuse it with its own personality.

Similar to how the military's core values are used to rally the troops, the same must be said about your core values. They need to convey "this is how we do business here," establishing your left and right lateral limits for your team to operate within. If your clients, customers, and team members have a problem with it, that's okay, because then you know they are not a good fit for your company.

It is that simple.

When I started building IRONBOUND Media, I leaned heavily into establishing our core values, even though I was a one man show at the time. The previous year, I'd established the core values for IRONBOUND Boxing, and they worked wonders for us as a brand, allowing me to develop a brand playbook, a mini-book that tells the IRONBOUND Boxing story. With our values finally in place, I felt confident to officially stand up a board of directors, and during our first board meeting I briefed them on our core values. For the first time, it was as if IRONBOUND Boxing was a living and breathing entity.

EXAMPLE OF CORE VALUES

The following are IRONBOUND Media's core values with a detailed description of each. It's important you explain each value in detail, internally to your team and externally to customers and stakeholders. I recommend having between three to five core values. Anything more and you risk diluting each individual one's importance. Additionally, for every core value listed, you have to constantly ask yourself and your team whether or not you're living up to them.

To find out what your core values are, I recommend starting here: start by listing the traits and characteristics you hope to cultivate at your company. Below are ours at IRONBOUND Media:

Don't be afraid to start ugly: Mastery is built through countless hours of constant practice and repetition. In order to achieve mastery, you have to start with the understanding that you will get better over time. Embrace the growth mindset, and understand we all start ugly sometimes.

Never stop learning: You must be a master of your craft. You may not have all the answers, but you know where to find them. You need to be open to receiving and constantly seeking feedback. Read books and articles, listen to podcasts and audiobooks, and always look for new opportunities to grow and learn. Be a subject matter expert. That requires you to stay up to date on all relevant trends, as well as processes and systems for constantly improving your performance.

Protect the asset: We believe in order to reach your fullest potential, you need to ensure you're cultivating your mental, physical, and spiritual self. This means getting rest, taking care of your body through exercise, nutrition, and sleep, and nurturing your soul through reading, writing, or whatever you need to cultivate the spirit. You are the asset, and you must ensure you're taking care of yourself at all times.

Discipline equals freedom: In order to avoid stress and burnout, you have to embrace a culture of disciplined thought and disciplined action. Rather than focus on executing a lot of things poorly, strive to focus on a few things and execute them exceptionally well with discipline.

Lift as you climb: We don't want to live in a world where we're the only ones on the mountain top. We must constantly help others learn and grow alongside us. Whether giving back to the community, veterans, or your industry, embrace a mindset of helping others.

BOLD BELIEFS

Bold beliefs allow you to stand out from the pack and shout to the world who you are, what you stand for, and how you view your industry. Imagine climbing to the top of a mountain while carrying your brand's flag with you.

Once you reach the top and plant it into the ground, if you were to shout your company's bold beliefs from the top of your lungs, what would you say?

A great place to start is to write down what you believe.

For example, at IRONBOUND Boxing, we believe the following:

- Boxing changes lives.
- Inner-city boxing gyms are an untapped resource for cultivating and nourishing youth and young adults in low-income communities across the country.
- Eliminating barriers of entry to boxing training so youth and young adults can train for free.
- The country is facing a public health problem driven, in part, by the rising cost of fitness in America. The poorest quartile of the population gets about half the exercise as the wealthiest. Our gyms can change that.

Part of building a brand is having a clear understanding of who you are for, but more importantly, who you are not for. You know that from identifying who your perfect customer is in Chapter 5. Now is where your bold beliefs come in. If they don't believe in what you do and how you view the world, that's okay, they are not your perfect customer, and it is better to find out sooner rather than later.

BUILDING YOUR BRAND AROUND YOUR PERFECT CUSTOMER

With a clearly defined core purpose, core values, and bold beliefs, the next step in the process is to revisit your perfect customer and align your messaging and positioning around them.

For example, let's say you sell handcrafted and plant-based skin care products. You believe in environmental sustainability and donate 10 percent of your profits to environmental causes.

You want to align yourself with a perfect customer who also believes in sustainability, utilizes plant-based skin care products, and is willing to pay a premium for your products.

The simplest way to do so is by crafting a compelling one-liner, which includes your perfect customer, and placing it front and center on your website and any other marketing or promotional materials. This one-liner must be repeated by every member of your team as well as communicated verbally by those who refer you.

For example, "We create handcrafted and plant-based skin care products for business professionals who believe in sustainability."

Who is the perfect customer?: Business professionals who believe in sustainability. (You can niche down even more, i.e., lawyers.)

What do you do?: Create handcrafted and plant-based skincare products.

What's the problem you solve?: Connecting customers with plant-based products

CONNECT THE DOTS

The final step is to connect the dots on all of the above. And this is where your internal and external branding comes into play. You can start by placing your core purpose, core values, bold beliefs, and perfect customer on a single document. That way you can add to it later and also share it with any team members.

If you hire a graphic designer to help build your website and other marketing assets, share your document with them so they have a better understanding of your brand. The same goes for social media managers, copywriters, and anyone else working in marketing. It's important everyone understands your branding essentials. Then you can start to build upon them for your logo and website.

Unfortunately, too many BVEs do things the other way around and start building their website and marketing materials first before they've spent time developing their brand. Not you. Now that you better understand how to build a brand, you won't put the cart before the horse.

BUILDING BRAND AWARENESS

You are probably saying to yourself, "Mike this all sounds great, but once we do all of this how do we go about building brand awareness?"

When it comes to building brand awareness, start identifying the channels and mediums that allow you to communicate with your perfect customer. This doesn't mean hiding behind the internet or social media.

While social media is a great platform for nourishing and engaging clients, don't make the mistake of solely relying on it for brand awareness, especially when you're first launching. Always remember, the best brand awareness comes from paying clients and customers!

However, when you do use social media, I suggest focusing on the platforms your perfect customer uses most frequently. Post valuable content consistently to establish what you want to be known for, and look for opportunities to engage with them directly through one-on-one reach out.

You can learn about them, start conversations, and position yourself for success to do business with them. From there, you should figure out ways to activate your clients and turn them into brand evangelists. We'll discuss this more in detail in Chapter 10, "How to Acquire Your First Ten Customers and Beyond."

Visit BlackVeteranEntrepreneurs.com/BuildYourBrand to download your Build Your Brand worksheet.

HOW THIS APPLIES TO YOU:
- Before you make a logo, website, or anything else, start by defining your "why."
- Define your company's values and bold beliefs, getting everything down on paper.
- Make sure your values align with your perfect customer and how you do business.
- Build brand awareness through direct one-on-one reach out.

ADDITIONAL RESOURCES:

READ

- *BE 2.0 (Beyond Entrepreneurship 2.0): Turning Your Business into an Enduring Great Company* by Jim Collins
- *Building a StoryBrand: Clarify Your Message So Customers Will Listen* by Donald Miller

LISTEN

- *The Transition* podcasts: "How To Build A Brand"
- *Dog Whistle Branding*: "Establishing Your Brand's Why With Commander's Intent"

7

POSITION YOURSELF
OR BE POSITIONED

"I am the greatest, I said that even before I knew I was."

—MUHAMMAD ALI

If there's one weakness amongst the veteran entrepreneurial community, it's our inability to effectively position our products or services in a way that differentiates us from the competition, captures demand, and drives revenue.

Don't get me wrong, there are some very successful veteran-owned brands, BVE or otherwise, that have managed to stand out from the crowd and become highly profitable.

But by and large, after participating in upward of eight to ten entrepreneur programs and talking with well over five hundred veteran entrepreneurs, struggling with positioning is a recurring theme.

It's not our fault: In the military, we were taught leadership and mental toughness, not positioning! Before you launch your product or service, you need to pick between one of the following three options:

Compete in an existing market, which I don't recommend, especially for first-time founders.

Niche down in a profitable market with existing demand, such as digital marketing, and carve out your own niche, i.e., digital marketing for professional service firms in the New Jersey area.

Design and dominate your own market category, which is my personal favorite but not for the faint at heart.

Of all the options above, niching down and category design are the best courses of action for BVEs.

TORCH WARRIORWEAR

In the summer of 2021, Haley Marie McClain Hill, Air Force officer and NFL cheerleader, woke up late for work one day while still wearing her bodysuit and jeans from the night before.

Bodysuits are comfortable and a civilian wardrobe staple for some women. However, there weren't any on the market for women to wear in uniform that fit regulation undershirt's color and cut.

While getting out of her bodysuit and into her uniform, Haley came up with a new business idea.

What if there was a bodysuit for female armed service members that was within military regulation?

A few days later she started doing some research and officially launched TORCH Warriorwear, an LA-based clothing brand for modern day women warriors, focusing on armed service members and first responders.

Haley created the new category of "warriorwear" that is like athleisure but for women in the military, first responders, and other female-centric career fields and even sports such as Jiu Jitsu. Rather than be stuck with brands like Nike and Under Armour for high performance undergarments, female warriors have a brand specifically for them.

Haley's vision for TORCH is to create wardrobes free from constraints and shapelessness and are tweaked with tactical accents. As a former Penn State cheerleader who managed to continue her cheerleading career in the NFL while on active duty, she always loved fashion. Haley understands firsthand the importance of looking good and feeling good, and through TORCH, she aims to empower other military women to do so.

Since launching in 2021, TORCH has generated over $80,000 in revenue and is growing. She bootstrapped the company and is working diligently to build out the category of warriorwear, distinguishable from traditional apparel.

Haley wants women in the military to maintain their femininity while being fearless in the pursuit of what sets their soul on fire. Her vision is to create a company to inspire women with tactical but comfortable uniform options they can't imagine living without.

DEMAND IS EVERYTHING

A great idea doesn't guarantee success, especially if there's no market for what you're offering. Although TORCH is still in its early days, Haley identified a strong market pool because women warriors are already spending money on bodysuits and uniforms, so the potential for a strong demand is there.

I often reflect back to early 2018 shortly after I began teaching corporate boxing classes under the IRON-BOUND umbrella and was barely keeping my head afloat. One of the many reasons I struggled so hard was because I didn't do the best job of positioning myself in a market with a strong demand.

While companies were increasingly spending money in the corporate wellness sector, boxing itself wasn't a priority and sure as heck didn't demand a premium rate, at least not nearly as much as I'm able to generate now through IRONBOUND Media with our brand strategy and podcast production services.

At the time, the going rate for on-site trainers in the NYC metro area ranged between $70 and $250 per session. When I launched I was only bringing in a $100 or so a session. I didn't know how to sell, and I was afraid of charging a premium rate because I didn't have any market validation that companies would pay it, or at least pay me!

It also didn't help that I was terrified of sales.

For almost a year, I felt like I was climbing an uphill battle every time I spoke with a warm prospect, which oftentimes was a twenty-year-old office or community manager responsible for wellness programming.

To be perfectly honest, our classes were viewed as a "vitamin," something that's a "nice to have," as opposed to a "painkiller," something they couldn't live without.

Don't get me wrong, while there are some executives who are actively looking for boxing instructors for themselves and their team, by and large, they aren't spending a premium on it, at least not in the corporate wellness sector. I discovered this the hard way up until the pandemic put me out of my own misery and forced me to explore a new business model altogether.

If you remember nothing else, remember this when it comes to positioning.

You can be the best entrepreneur in the world and have an amazing team behind you. If the market demand is not there for what you are offering, you are going to fail or, even worse, extend your business into a long, miserable journey, fighting for margin monthly with no end in sight.

In his article, "Business is like surfing," Justin Jackson, IndieMaker and Serial Tech entrepreneur, writes, "In the beginning, it probably doesn't make sense to spend much time thinking about positioning, sales, and marketing. These things are important, but only if you've first identified the right opportunity. The way you position your board is important once you're riding a wave. But, positioning won't help your product if there's no demand."

He goes on to say how, "as entrepreneurs, we respond to existing demand, we don't create it." The market should already be "pulling" for what you're building; the demand should already exist.

POSITIONING FIRST, MARKETING SECOND

Over the last few years, several books and articles have been written about positioning by experts such as April Dunford, author of *Obviously Awesome: How to Nail Product Positioning so Customers Get It, Buy It, Love It*, and Arielle Jackson, marketer in residence at First Round Capital, a seed stage venture capital firm that invests in technology start-ups.

Both April and Arielle are positioning experts who have worked with hundreds of entrepreneurs over the years, consistently emphasizing the importance of setting context when it comes to positioning a product or service in the market.

In her blog, April states, "Customers are not experts on *your* product (or services). They will naturally try to quickly match your product's most obvious features with a market category they already understand. If your best features are difficult to wrap their minds around, they will ignore them and focus on the easy to understand stuff. The result often places a really innovative product in a category it can never win."

Essentially, April is saying if you want to avoid commoditization, you have to own your narrative and positioning. Help your customers understand why you matter to them, or you risk becoming commoditized and ending up another nameless brand.

To avoid that, you need to do the work ahead of time, not only positioning your product or services in the eyes of your customer, but ensuring you are identifying a market where they are already spending money or have market validation that they will in the future!

From there, you need to craft a positioning thesis, a rough draft of how you explain your company's value proposition, and test it with customers. The more customers you talk and do business with, the better understanding you'll have.

NICHE DOWN IN AN EXISTING MARKET
The majority of BVEs will benefit from simply niching down in an existing market with a strong market demand and redirecting the demand to them.

In *Category Pirates*, a paid newsletter that teaches you how to think like a category designer, the authors refer to this strategy as "Damming the Demand." Damming the demand is looking for market opportunities where your perfect customer is already spending money. Rather than competing for that demand, create a category that dams it to you, similar to damming a river.

Start by looking for niches where you have a tactical advantage, such as in my case, being a Black veteran entrepreneur who writes educational content for other BVEs.

Rob Walling, author of *Start Small, Stay Small: A Developer's Guide to Launching a Startup*, shares, "The genius of niches is they are too small for large competitors, allowing a nimble entrepreneur the breathing room to focus on an underserved audience. Once you've succeeded in that niche, you can leverage your success to establish credibility for your business to move into larger markets."

For example, IRONBOUND Media's perfect customers are growth stage veteran-owned business owners. Unfortunately, at the time when I launched the company, many of them weren't sold on podcasting, let alone willing to spend money on it. Rather than merely positioning myself as a podcast production company, I positioned us as marketing and branding experts. Although veteran-owned businesses weren't spending money on podcasting, they were spending a hell of a lot of money marketing and branding and were frustrated with their results at the time.

One of my clients was spending $3,500 a month on a social media marketing specialist before I started working with him. He received little to no return for that investment.

Once he got into podcasting, we were able to dam the demand for him, and he got the results he needed.

If you plan on launching a consumer packaged goods (CPG) company, selling items such as coffee or tea, niche down in an underserved market with strong buying potential, .i.e., matcha tea for female lawyers in the NYC metro area.

Once you niche and dam the demand, go the extra step and name your niche and claim it as your own.

CREATE YOUR OWN CATEGORY

Designing and creating your own category takes guts. It's an audacious business strategy, with the opportunity for the most upside.

In the *Harvard Business Review* article, "Why It Pays to Be a Category Creator," Eddie Yoon and Linda Deeken state,

To find out just how lucrative category creation can be, our company examined *Fortune*'s lists of the 100 fastest-growing US companies from 2009 to 2011. We found that the thirteen companies that were instrumental in creating their categories accounted for 53 percent of incremental revenue growth and 74 percent of incremental market capitalization growth over those three years. The message is clear: Category creators experience much faster growth and receive much higher valuations from investors than companies bringing only incremental innovations to market.

What does this mean for BVEs?

Rather than trying to compete in existing markets, BVEs should do the opposite and position themselves as a category of one. A word of caution before you begin: Creating a new category is no small feat and requires a different level of thinking. It requires you to think outside the present and envision a reimagined future.

I first learned about the process of category design from the book, *Play Bigger: How Pirates, Dreamers, and Innovators, Create, and Dominate Markets.* The book describes category design as "a business strategy that focuses on creating a new marketing category, which can then be monetized and monopolized before competitors can enter the space. By establishing a new niche that is free of competition, your company has an excellent chance of dominating it."

Based on the authors' research of some of the world's most successful companies, they determined that category kings own 70 percent of market share in any category, and if you're not a category king, you're competing for the bottom 24 percent of the category along with every other competitor in the space.

Think of social media. Facebook is the category king. The same can be said for Apple with smart phones or Salesforce with customer resource management (CRM). Category kings are all around us.

In order to be a category king, BVEs need to go through the following category design process below:
- Develop a differentiated point-of-view
- Frame your category

- Name your category
- Claim your category

DEVELOPING A DIFFERENTIATED POINT-OF-VIEW

Category kings create categories from scratch, leveraging a differentiated point-of-view, which details how they see the world and their industry, which contrasts heavily with status quo.

This means being able to take yourself out of the present and envision a reimagined future in your new marketing category.

For example, right now, BVEs are underfunded and underestimated, no different than the rest of our nation's Black entrepreneurs. I envision a reimagined future where rather than relying on others to fund us, we fund ourselves, starting our own venture capital funds to invest in one another and our communities. I envision conferences specifically designed for BVEs, where we no longer have to feel like we're one of one and have panels featuring us in our own skin; where we can let our guard down and learn from each other how to survive and thrive as Black veteran entrepreneurs. I envision a world where the Black community looks to the BVEs to invest in them.

That is the power of a differentiated point of view: It goes beyond the surface level and forces you to think differently about the world.

In the words of Antoine de Saint-Exupéry, author of *The Little Prince*, "If you want to build a ship, don't drum up the men to gather wood, divide the work, and give orders. Instead, teach them to yearn for the vast and endless sea."

Dope Coffee's point of view is Black people love coffee, and they can be their full selves while drinking it, listening to R&B or hip hop music, and having dope conversations about race, culture, and business. Nothing against Starbucks or other specialty coffee brands, but Dope Coffee sees the world through a different lens. A Dope Coffee shop resembles more of a record store, or lounge with hip hop music, than it does a modern day Starbucks.

Before you can even begin designing your category, you have to lean into your point of view and convey how you see the world, specifically, how it contrasts what others see today.

Once you've developed your differentiated point-of-view, the next step is to frame your category.

Frame your category
Framing your category is the equivalent of "shaping the battlefield" and choosing the turf that you want to engage the enemy on. Only this isn't war—this is business.

When you think about your perfect customer and the problems they are facing, such as being in need of instant pain relief, or not having access to a community of founders and investors who look like them, where do you see a market opportunity?

Recently, a fellow Marine and entrepreneur, Scott Patterson, started a company called Tumble. Tumble introduces smart laundry into the multi-family ecosystem. Scott identified how archaic laundry is, despite the opportunities tech presents. Every year, people are spending billions of dollars in coins on laundry at apartment buildings, laundromats, and any other shared locations. Scott realized the market opportunity for tech-enabled laundry machines, allowing users to pay for the laundry services via an app while also tracking when their laundry is complete.

Between the lack of tech in this market, the amount of money being spent on laundry, and the inefficiency of modern laundry, Scott framed the perfect problem for Tumble to build a category and be a category king.

Name your category
When it comes time to name your category, you want to get creative and think outside of the box. Choose words that convey your differentiated point of view. You'll have to do a little wordsmithing.

Over the last few years, I've designed multiple categories, the first, Dog Whistle Branding (DWB), a marketing and branding category specifically for veteran-owned businesses. I designed the category using the book, *Play Bigger*, along with *Traversing The Traction Gap* by Bruce Cleveland. I also designed the category of Courage Academies, which I'm in the process of introducing into the youth development ecosystem as I'm writing this book.

Courage Academies are a combination of boxing gyms and small business incubators meant to build courage and resilience of youth and young adults in the inner-city. I came up with the name to convey the same courage it takes to step inside a boxing ring is the same courage it takes to start a business. I know personally because I've done both!

I created Dog Whistle Branding to challenge veteran-owned businesses to view their brands as dog whistles, and every time they blow on them, such as sending a newsletter, releasing a podcast episode, or posting on their blog, their sole purpose is to get the attention of their perfect customer.

Dog, whistle, and branding are simply three words I managed to pair together to create a category of one. I did the same process with BVE.

Think like a superhero
If you're having trouble coming up with a name, just imagine your brand is a superhero. Naming a superhero is the same as naming your category: Think about Spider-Man, Iron Man, or even the Incredible Hulk! Even take Marvel Founder Stan Lee's lead and get creative!

The key is creating a name in such a way that your perfect customer doesn't have to guess what the category is about.

Is it hard to determine what Black veteran entrepreneur means? I highly doubt it! I came up with the name after a simple internet search and realized there was little to no business content specifically targeting BVEs. So I've decided to create the category for BVEs such as myself and write this book to frame, name, and claim it!

In order to stake claim to your category, you have to evangelize it relentlessly.

When you first start, no one is going to know about your category, let alone how to navigate within it. This is where you control the narrative and expectations.

Brands make the mistake of evangelizing and promoting themselves instead of their category. All of your marketing and branding should be around promoting the category, whether on podcasts, blog series, or public speaking.

When someone thinks of your company, the first thing they should think of is the category, which will naturally result in brand awareness. Category kings are always top of mind when it comes to your perfect customer.

As a boxing coach, whenever I think of purchasing equipment for my kids at IRONBOUND Boxing, the first company that pops into my mind is Everlast.

Everlast has been around for over a hundred years and are the category kings of boxing equipment globally. They've reached such a point of market dominance that they are able to focus their marketing efforts around branding alone, promoting the story and what it means to be a boxer.

What are you doing to stay top of mind for your perfect customer?

Category kings are evangelist. They relentlessly promote the category, even launching conferences, workshops, and certifications.

Who knows, in the future maybe we'll have a conference for BVEs to come learn and fellowship. (I'm already creating laptop stickers and apparel, so be on the lookout!)

PROMOTE THE CATEGORY, NOT THE BRAND

Whether you decide to niche down in an existing category or create your own, when it comes to marketing your company, don't make the mistake of over promoting your brand and not enough time promoting and evangelizing the market category.

Be ruthless about educating your market about the value of your market category. Teach everything you know and let that drive demand to your products or services.

Visit www.BlackVeteranEntrepreneurs.com/Positioning-Worksheets to download your worksheets to walk through the topics covered in this chapter.

HOW THIS APPLIES TO YOU:
- Focus on positioning from the very beginning and decide if you're going to compete, niche down, or create a new category.
- Craft a positioning thesis and start talking to customers as soon as possible to better learn how your company is positioned in their mind.

- Don't be afraid to niche down and dam the demand!
- If you have the guts to create a new category, follow the category design process listed above.

ADDITIONAL RESOURCES:

READ

- *Play Bigger: How Pirates, Dreamers, and Innovators Create and Dominate Markets* by Al Ramadan, Dave Peterson, Christopher Lochhead, and Kevin Maney
- *Obviously Awesome: How to Nail Product Positioning so Customers Get It, Buy It, Love It* by April Dunford
- *Category Pirates* by Christopher Lochhead, Edie Yoon, and Nicholas Cole

LISTEN

- *Lochhead on Marketing*, hosted by Christopher Lochhead
- *Dog Whistle Branding*: "A Veterans Guide To Category Design"

8

CREATE A MENU OF PRODUCTS AND SERVICES

"The best entrepreneurs have found a way to serve others and as a result discover their greatest fulfillment."

—GEORGE FOREMAN

Before you kick off your go-to market (GTM) campaign, the moment you launch and start driving revenue, you're going to need a list of products and services to offer to potential customers.

Having a list makes it easier for customers to do business with you and allows you and your team to focus on a limited number of specific offerings.

I don't know about you, but whenever I visit a coffee shop, one of the first things I look at is their menu. I'm a mocha latte kind of guy myself, but occasionally I like to spice things up with a dirty chai latte every now and then. The nice thing about coffee shop menus is how easy it is for me to see their offerings and make a purchase.

On the other extreme, I think about menus at diners, which are often packaged with pages and pages of different food, ranging from breakfast, lunch, and dinner. I can only imagine how difficult it must be to serve all these different options, including training the staff on how to cook them. The sheer volume of different offerings overwhelm me.

To prevent this from happening to your clients and to streamline your sales process, I recommend finding a balance with a simplified list of offerings, ranging from one to three products, and building a recurring sales process around it. Remember, in the early days of your venture, you're just trying to validate your business model and get repeatable sales. You can expand your offerings in the future, but for now the goal is to focus and make things easier for your perfect customers to do business with you.

Remember, if you are not selling and generating revenue, you do not have a business, you have a hobby. I remember the first time someone said those words to me. It felt like a punch in the gut. Looking back, I know they were right. If you want to build a business, you must have something to offer customers. Nonprofit organizations are no exception.

GREEN CLEAN AUTO SPA

When John Hunter launched Green Clean Auto Spa in 2015, an eco-friendly alternative car wash in Jacksonville, North Carolina, customers had six packages to choose from.

While on active duty studying building construction at Auburn University, as part of an commissioning program to become a Marine officer, John came up with the idea to open a car washing business. He originally enlisted in the Marine Corps and later earned an opportunity to become an officer after a competitive selection process amongst his peers.

One day while driving through a local car wash, John was struck by the new technology, including robots and machines, which allowed car washes to operate with a limited number of staff. Intrigued by the market potential and the opportunity to operate a self-sustaining business with limited employees, he began vigorously studying the car wash industry.

He attended industry conferences and went through training on how to operate and manage a car wash business while on active duty. After returning from a deployment to Afghanistan, John finally had the courage to launch his own car wash. He worked hard and secured a bank loan to purchase an old and run-down car wash and ran it as-is. A year later, he was able to secure a loan to completely renovate the facility as well as upgrade the equipment, officially launching Green Clean Auto Spa.

We started with six different washes in 2015. We are currently at four wash packages. In 2023, I will go to three menu items. Our goal is to focus on good, better, best menu packages to make the decision for consumers go faster. We want a clean, uncluttered menu that allows customers to decide quickly. I have found that the more options customers have, the more time it takes for them to decide."

John had to decide if he wanted to be the low, middle, or high car wash space when it came to pricing.

I knew if we were expensive, we had to deliver on customer service amongst other things. If we were the low price guys we could get away with not having the cleanest cars. Starting off, I decided to be in-line with my competitors until I had a good foundation and got training where we wanted.

Once he became established, he gradually started increasing the price of their bottom packages in order to increase the overall average ticket per customer.

Today, his company is the most expensive car washing service in the area, but they also have the service and product to support the costs.

Customers care about service... if you provide a great service, they will pay. In many instances, you can win if the service is stellar with a mediocre product. Fortunately, we provide great service and a great product.

Today, John operates seven facilities with several in the pipeline for construction. As the company has evolved, so has its pricing packages.

I believe it is a constantly evolving area that you have to continuously improve and change as the customer changes.

DEVELOP YOUR OFFERINGS

You need to learn how to package your offerings in a way that, each with a specific price point, makes it easy for your perfect customer to do business with you. Keep things simple, and start with no more than three different offerings.

I know what you might be thinking. You have grand ambitions for your venture, and three products does not seem like enough. Especially for BVEs on the creative side who intend to launch an apparel company, maker products, and various other businesses.

However, trust me when I tell you this, in the early days of your venture you cannot afford to invest in giant overhead and operating costs. You need to be as efficient as possible. You will achieve success faster by selling one to three key products until you reach profitability and then gradually introduce more offerings later on. Trying to create and deliver anything more than three before you successfully validate your business model, with little to no money in the bank account, is a recipe for disaster.

Your initial menu should include:
- A list of all products and services
- Specific price points for each item/package
- Features and add-ons for each offering

Think about your time in the military.

We learned that before committing an entire force to attack the enemy, you send out a scouting team and gather information on the enemy. This team is usually no more than a squad size element of twelve to fifteen Marines, or a single reconnaissance airplane. Once you get eyes on and validate your assumptions, then you can brief the rest of your unit to attack. Anything else is doomed to fail.

The same patience must be applied in business.

KEEP IT SIMPLE

Going to market with one to three products gives you an opportunity to beta test them while keeping your overhead low. In addition, it also allows you to focus and get good at selling your core products and services.

For example, let's say you are a solo founder, and you decide to start a consumer packaged goods company that sells homemade taco sauce. Once you decide to launch and go public with your venture, you offer ten different flavors to your customers. As a result, this means you have to purchase ten different types of ingredients to accommodate each flavor and create different labels, bottle sizes, and anything else. You have essentially ten-times your workload before ten-times your revenue!

Not to mention, each flavor will require its own unique selling proposition and messaging. Convincing someone to purchase your chipotle flavor is different than getting them to purchase the barbecue one.

How much easier would it be to focus on three bottles of taco sauce as opposed to ten?

Often times, we make business more complicated than it needs to be because we focus on the wrong things. In the early days, the goal is about getting really good at selling and delivering value to customers. Rather than adding more complexity to your venture early on, the goal is to keep it as simple as possible. When I launched IRONBOUND Media, I started off offering bronze, silver, and gold production packages with our lowest price point starting at $2,500 and the highest at $7,500. This is not to say you cannot modify your packages later, should you choose too. This is just a good starting point to go to the market confidently.

On the nonprofit side of the house, you can offer donation packages, in a similar fashion, and focus on obtaining a certain number of donors for each package in order to drive revenue for your organization. Set a donation amount to each package and send it out to your network.

A question that comes up constantly is:
"How do you know what to charge for your products and services?"

What is nice about this method is that it would allow you to leverage market-based feedback, what's working and what's not working, based on what people are purchasing. For example, I didn't know what to initially charge for my podcasts services, so rather than overthinking things, I offered three different price points to the first potential prospect I came across. When they immediately chose our platinum package, which at the time was $7,500, I realized I wasn't charging enough and readjusted my price offerings.

The next time I was in front of a prospect, I updated our price point for the platinum package by $10,000. When the next prospect immediately purchased the platinum package again, I realized I could still charge more.

Most people will not admit this, but it is an on-going game to figure out pricing, based on what prospects are willing to pay and how much your value is worth. As you get better at delivering value to your clients over time, you'll develop a strong client portfolio and brand reputation and confidently be able to charge more for your offerings.

Regardless of what industry you're in, whether professional services, CPG, or physical products, you can still follow the process above.

This is not to say you can't offer more options in the future. This is simply keeping with the five-stages of small business growth during the early stages when your sole focus should be validating your business model and obtaining predictable monthly recurring revenue.

Visit www.BlackVeteranEntrepreneurs.com/PricingResources for additional pricing resources and formulas to ensure your pricing covers your expenses, taxes, and more so you know you will make a profit.

HOW THIS APPLIES TO YOU:
- Think big but start small by creating a menu of no more than three products or services.

- Learn to package and productize everything, whether you are a service based business, nonprofit, or CPG.
- Assign price points to each of your offerings and adjust your prices based on what your perfect customer is purchasing.
- Gradually increase your price points over time until you have a better understanding of the value you offer and what people are willing to pay for it.
- Keep things simple.

ADDITIONAL RESOURCES:

READ

- *Disciplined Entrepreneurship: 24 Steps to a Successful Start-up 1st Edition*, Chapter 16: "Your Pricing Framework," by Bill Aulet

LISTEN

- *The Transition* podcasts: "How to Create a Menu of Products and Services"

9

THE CUSTOMER ACTIVATION CYCLE

"Great leaders are almost always great simplifiers who can cut through the argument debate and doubt to offer a solution everybody can understand."

—COLIN POWELL

Before you catch a fish, you better know what to do with it. Do you put it in the cooler? Do you throw it back in the water and let it swim upstream? What's the plan? If you don't know, neither will anyone else.

Taking the time to develop a customer activation cycle, a step by step process your perfect customer goes through before purchasing, is a must-have for BVEs. Not having a customer activation cycle (CAC) is equivalent to catching a fish and not knowing what to do with it once you have it.

In business we are not catching fish; however, we are dealing with real people who have problems that need to be solved. Your goal is to help them solve it, and you need a plan to demonstrate your ability to do so.

TRUEFIKTION

While attending business school at Northwestern University's Kellogg School of Business, Army veteran and West Point graduate Stephane Manuel came up with the idea for TrueFiktion, an educational technology company that builds comics, curriculum, and community around the untold stories of marginalized groups.

During Stephane's 2015 deployment to Afghanistan, the city of Baltimore, Maryland, erupted in racial unrest following the death of Freddie Gray, an unarmed Black man who died in police custody. Ferguson, Missouri, went through similar unrest the year prior only after the death of Michael Brown, another unarmed Black man killed in St. Louis, Missouri.

As he fought for his country abroad, Stephane began to question why he was fighting for freedom and equality overseas when unarmed Black men were dying at home.

"I did not know how to process what was happening in my community," Manuel said in an interview with the Segal Design Institute at Northwestern University's Kellogg School of Management.

American history is framed as a monolithic, uninterrupted story of progress. So when I looked at current events, especially civil rights, I didn't have the tools or frameworks to understand why so many issues were occurring. I was always bothered by the fact that I didn't know how we got to the problems we face today. If I didn't know, how could I not take any action to fix issues at home? I shouldn't have left high school without knowing how to fix issues in my community and the historical reasons for those issues.

After leaving active duty to attend business school, Stephane began exploring different business models to support the Black community.

Now through TrueFiktion, Stephane is able to bridge the gap for other young men and women of color, working with teachers and administrators at charter schools, by utilizing design thinking to develop a comic book series to discuss difficult subject matters for students, such as segregation, racism, and other troubling history from our past.

We are using comics as a medium to drive empathy around multiple perspectives of history and help people deal with the complexity of history... We often think history is a series of facts, but there are a lot of things we will never know for sure, and sometimes two things can be true at the same time when it comes to history.

TrueFiktion's perfect customer is a charter school principal or director of education and curriculum, with a budget upward of $15,000 to afford their services.

TrueFiktion's CAC is fairly straightforward. Stephane uses multiple events to drive a potential customer to book a demo with his organization. He publishes case studies on using his products, provides thought leadership around using comics to engage students of color, conducts webinars on culturally responsive teaching methods, and attends conferences where he provides professional development for teachers. All of the activities drive his list of warm leads. Once Stephane identifies a warm lead, his goal is to book an initial thirty-minute call with them to learn more about the challenges the school faces, followed by a demo of TrueFiktion's products and workshops to secure a formal engagement.

As a solo founder, Stephane doesn't have a budget to hire a marketing team yet, so he relies heavily on the CAC to drive revenue and give him the ability to quickly qualify leads. He's launched multiple pilot programs with charter schools in time and is excited about the future.

SIMPLE, NOT EASY

Although the CAC sounds simple, it is imperative that you map out your process beforehand and not leave it to assumptions. Mapping it out allows you to maximize opportunities within the cycle, such as sending marketing materials to prospects before each stage.

I first learned about the customer activation cycle from Bill Watkins, my business coach, and have read various versions of it over the years. Essentially, a CAC begins from the moment a prospect expresses interest in doing business with you, and continues as you map out how to convert them into a paying client/customer, and eventually becomes a superfan, in the most efficient way possible. Honestly, a strong customer activation cycle is all you need to get your first ten customers.

At a bare minimum, a customer activation cycle should include three phases:
- Pre-purchase activation
- Purchase activation
- Post-purchase activation

With a CAC, you want to start mapping out the sequence of events a customer will go through to the point of initial contact, through the sales process, and beyond.

For example:
Let's say you are selling an online product. Your CAC might look like something similar below:

Pre-purchase:
- The prospect visits your website.
- The prospect begins searching different product offerings.
- The prospect presses "purchase."

Purchase:
- Prospect enters credit card information.
- Prospect purchases the product, turning into a customer.

Post-purchase
- Customer enters database.
- Receives "Thank You" email for purchasing.
- Receives weekly newsletter from the company.

Although this process seems straight forward, the reality is prospects visit websites every day and do not make a purchase, which is why once you map out the process, you need to think more intentionally about each phase.

For the pre-purchase phase: What's the prospect looking at once they're on the website? Is there a chat bot they can talk with? Is there an FAQ that answers common questions? Is there an email capture to join your list?

Being on the page is only part of the process.

What's the layout of the page, and how are the different offerings presented? Are they able to save the product in a cart and come back later?

Before they purchase, is there any kind of brand guarantee on the purchasing, i.e., offering a refund or discount on future products if they don't like it?

Is there anything on the credit card page that could make them second guess the purchase? If so, how can you overcome it?

Finally, once they do decide to purchase the product, is there any follow up? Are you adding them to a database?

Although this can seem overwhelming at first, it's a necessary process to think through if you plan on driving revenue. If you run a service based business, such as me, your customer activation cycle may look slightly different.

IRONBOUND'S CUSTOMER ACTIVATION CYCLE

At IRONBOUND Media, we first identify our warm leads, i.e., veteran-owned small businesses who generate up to $1 million a year in revenue. I've done my best to establish myself as an authority in the field of marketing and branding for veteran-owned businesses, so I get a constant stream of warm leads, thanks to my podcasts, social media, and referrals from my network.

Once someone emails me or my team expressing interests in our services, I take them through the following process:

- Pre-purchase
  - Prospect identifies as a warm lead.
  - Conduct a brand probe with prospect (our initial engagement).
  - Select Prospect selects a production package and becomes a client.

- Purchase:
  - Receive initial down payment.
  - Kick off project.
  - Execute project.

- Post-purchase:
  - Send weekly newsletter to client.
  - Invite client on the *Dog Whistle Branding* podcast.
  - Send the client a swag bag.

After we identify the warm lead we secure an initial meeting and offer them an opportunity to go through our brand probe. The brand probe allows us to demonstrate our value and give prospects a taste of what it would be like to work with my team and me. I've found this to be extremely effective when it comes to getting to know potential clients and building a rapport with them.

People do business with those they know, like, and trust. Giving them a taste of what it's like to work with you is a great start. If you are a product based business, share with them a sample of your work. If you are running a nonprofit, invite them to your facility or invite them to meet with some of your stakeholders, such as young athletes at the IRONBOUND Boxing Academy.

The options are limitless. The key is demonstrating value.

When it comes to my clients picking their package, I want to reinforce the importance of having an uncomplicated menu of products and services. You want to make the process as seamless as possible for them, so you need to know your price points ahead of time and be able to demonstrate them with confidence. It also makes it easier for clients and prospects to refer you to someone else when they have a clear understanding of your pricing and what you offer.

For service-based businesses, I am a big proponent of receiving a down payment for your services upfront. I have to give credit to where credit is due, of course. I learned the importance of charging upfront from my business coach, Bill. This might not work for every industry, but it is worth noting the importance of maintaining positive cash flow at any given time; otherwise, you risk running out of money.

When I first launched IRONBOUND Media, I was initially hesitant to invoice up front. I always assumed you did the work first, then received payment. Coming from the workforce, that's what I was accustomed to. Once I started invoicing up front, it gave me a better understanding of the caliber of clients I was looking for as perfect customers. I firmly believe business is still people to people. Business owners who are looking to do serious business with you understand the value you bring to the table and will pay a down payment. Since I started invoicing up front, I have not looked back.

By the time we reach the project kick off, this is where we get a time set on the calendar with the client to give them a plan of what to expect next and start creating their podcasts.

Regardless of what industry you are in, a solid customer activation cycle is a game changer. Your CAC will systematize your sales process and allow you to consistently convert prospects. At first, your CAC will serve as your initial marketing plan, combined with sales scrappiness, such as attending events and meeting people or sending emails to warm prospects. Once they respond, the goal is to push through your CAC.

As you earn more revenue, you will have more margin and a better understanding of who you're processing therefore you'll have a more effective marketing plan.

Visit www.BlackVeteranEntrepreneurs.com/CustomerActivationCycle to download your worksheet to establish your customer activation cycle

HOW THIS APPLIES TO YOU:

- Map out the step-by-step process to take a warm prospect into a paying customer.
- Share it internally with all team members.
- Think through how to minimize friction points at each stage of the process.
- Develop marketing assets to support each stage (menu of services, videos, FAQs, overview, etc.)

ADDITIONAL RESOURCES:

READ

- *The 1-Page Marketing Plan: Get New Customers, Make More Money, And Stand Out From The Crowd* by Allen Dib

LISTEN

- *Dog Whistle Branding*: "How To Convert Prospects into Paying Customers with a Customer Activation Cycle"

10

HOW TO ACQUIRE YOUR FIRST TEN CUSTOMERS AND BEYOND

"Success isn't about how much money you make; it's about the difference you make in people's lives."

—MICHELLE OBAMA

It is one thing to develop your business idea in the shadows, free from the visibility of doubters and naysayers, allowing yourself to avoid the reality of whether or not you have a viable business model. At some point, you have to step out into the light to face the market head on.

You don't know what you don't know. Fortunately, or unfortunately, everything up until your launch is all based on assumptions. But once you are able to get paying customers (or not), you will be able to leverage market-based feedback, a rapid based feedback loop generated from interactions with paying customers.

I am not talking about pitch competitions either. While they may be a great opportunity for getting feedback on your venture, when it comes to putting money in the bank account and validating your business model, they can be a distraction, especially in the early days when you are fighting to stay alive. With the exception of those of you who are swinging for the fences and launching a venture-backed startup, like AJ Yawn, founder & CEO of ByteChek.

Instead, focus your time, effort, and attention on getting profitable as soon as possible by selling to eager customers willing to pay you. Focus on your first ten customers, and *then* focus on scaling. The more customers you acquire, the more market-based feedback you are able to leverage in your positioning to make sure you have identified the perfect customer.

Back in 2018, when I came up with the for-profit model focused on corporate wellness for IRONBOUND Boxing, I had no idea who my perfect customer was. Instead of going to find out, I participated in countless pitch competitions and spent more time working on my pitch deck than I did talking to potential customers and on-boarding paying clients. While I got decent feedback, it was from a panel of judges and not customers.

I've said it once and I'll say it again, when it comes to validating a product or service in the market, nothing beats paying customers and generating revenue. Once you do, you'll figure it out real quick whether you have the makings of a real business.

It can feel nerve racking to go to market, a term used to describe launching a venture. But after you've developed your initial business plan, along with your brand and perfect customer, at some point you have to launch and bring your vision to life.

GRACE ELEYAE, INC.

Army veteran Emmanuel Eleyae knows more than a thing or two about taking brands from zero to one-hundred. Emmanuel is the owner of Eleyae Systems, a digital agency that scales brands from six figures a year to six figures a month in revenue, fast. He's also the cofounder of Grace Eleyae, Inc., a company that sells and designs headwear made of satin and silk.

Emmanuel began building brands after leaving the Army, first by helping his sister, Grace Eleyae, launch an e-commerce brand selling hair satin-lined caps to women, which the company refers to as Slaps. Grace came up with the idea after needing a cute way to protect her hair while on vacation to Kenya in the summer of 2013. The combination of dust and dry heat took its toll on her hair, inspiring her to create her own solution, the Slap. She recruited her brother to cofound the company with her, along with other members of her family, including her mom and younger sister. Their first customers came from friends and family.

In an interview with Klaviyo, an email marketing platform for e-commerce brands, Grace opens up about the company's origins. "I was taking sewing classes at night in 2013, but I didn't make the first Slap prototype for about a year. In February 2014, I showed it to friends and family, and they all said, 'This is great. I love it.' They became my first focus group. The first version was tiny—it looked like a skullcap—so my family helped me develop it to create the Slap we know now."

Next, Grace and Emmanuel launched the company on Etsy, selling their flagship Slap while simultaneously making the product in-house. Beyond those closest to them, Grace and Emmanuel clawed tooth and nail for every sale. They sent direct messages to potential customers online, set up shop at pop-ups, and did everything they could think of to drive revenue.

"For a while, we were still selling one or two Slaps a day on Etsy—we were rejoicing if we sold five in a day. Then, suddenly, we had twenty-five sales in one day. The next day, sales doubled."

The family's big break came when a YouTuber named CloudyApples, a lifestyle vlogger with a large following, named their flagship product "a must have" in her nighttime routine. Her endorsement of the product led to increased traffic to the site. Those customers purchased the product and left a review.

After realizing the impact of influencers, Emmanuel and his sister began targeting similar beauty bloggers, sending them their product, and this resulted in more and more rave reviews. With the influencers' endorsement, the Slap was brought into mainstream commerce.

They eventually moved beyond Etsy, setting up their own online e-commerce store. Unlike service businesses, such as consulting and marketing agencies, which can generate high margins with low overhead, e-commerce was a volume game with lots of overhead without healthy cash always available. Because of this, the Eleyae family had to work side jobs to pay the bills.

For the first three years, we grew time-times year-over-year, so we increased our revenue by about 1,000 percent each year. We went from around $80,000 our first year to $600,000 the next year and $5 million the year after. Now, we're making around $7.5 million a year in revenue.

The company has since rebranded into Grace Eleyae and is a million-dollar e-commerce brand. Since then, Emmanuel has used his knowledge and insights to help over thirty entrepreneurs build million-dollar and multi-million-dollar brands through his agency.

Emmanuel agrees the foundation of a go-to market strategy includes knowing your perfect customer and identifying the channels they frequent to engage with them. In the case of Grace Eleyae and after the success of the CloudyApples YouTube endorsement, they realized their perfect customer were social media influencers with a large audience of women.

From there it was about nourishing those relationships and activating them to help scale the brand to the next level.

In the early days of launching a venture, it is the founder's responsibility to find the perfect customer. Once you find a customer who's hungry for your product and is willing to pay you a premium, the goal is to find more just like them and scale from there.

THE FIRST TEN

Seth Godin, marketing expert and best-selling author, said it best in his blog entitled "The First Ten." Seth encourages founders to find ten people. "Ten people who trust you/respect you/need you/listen to you... Those ten people need what you have to sell, or want it. And if they love it, you win. If they love it, they'll each find ten more people (or a hundred or a thousand or, perhaps, just three). Repeat."

Like most things in life, as simple as this sounds, it is not easy.

Now that you have an understanding of how to think about going to market, I'm going to break things down for you at the tactical level. We will be leveraging the tools and frameworks we discussed in the previous chapters to help you close your first ten customers and beyond, including:
- Identifying your target market
- Honing in on your perfect customer avatar
- Filling your customer activation cycle
- Crafting a menu of products and service
- Adopting a relentless sales mentality

When it comes to generating revenue, a common approach is to start by building a marketing funnel with the goal of generating awareness, interests, and eventually sales. From the moment a prospect enters your funnel, the goal is to nurture them along the way so they eventually become paying customers.

The problem with this approach, particularly for Black veteran entrepreneurs, is by and large, it's ineffective in the early days. Some marketers may disagree with me, but for small businesses and early stage start-ups with limited funds in the bank account, the goal should be generating traction from day one.

Sales funnels are great for building a consistent sales pipeline after you have validated your business model, have a portfolio of clients, and have a strong understanding of your perfect customer. Unfortunately, in the early days, you need to generate momentum focusing on sales and do less generic marketing. You are going to have to get scrappy and go after prospects that are actively spending money to solve the problem your company addresses.

Paying customers make the venture real and give BVEs a better understanding of your unique selling proposition, allowing you to refine messaging to prospects, and create a more effective funnel. Before you can do any of this, you need customers! Paying customers are the only data that truly matters.

Many of us have friends and family who rely on us, and at a minimum we need to be able to cover our basic living expenses in order to ensure our families are taken care of. Sleeping on a buddy's couch while you build your business might sound good in a magazine or movie, but when it comes to real life, try explaining your living situation to your partner, especially those of you with kids.

During my entrepreneurial journey, I haven't come across too many BVEs who can afford to forgo profitability and live like monks for years, especially transitioning veterans.

I want you to generate revenue from the beginning. That starts by understanding your perfect customer and reverse engineering the process to engage with them.

At IRONBOUND Media, I work with veteran-owned businesses because I enjoy being around the veteran entrepreneurial ecosystem. Veterans are my tribe, and many of us already know, like, and trust each other, given our time in service. Not every community I come across is like this. If I wanted to open up a snowboard shop in Jackson Hole, Wyoming, I doubt I'd have as much success because I'm not immersed in the snowboarding culture around the area. That's not my tribe.

Additionally, what makes the veteran community unique to me is how much we care about one another's reputation and our willingness to not let each other down. Although I have aspirations to "punch above my weight" and expand services beyond the veteran space in an effort to generate more revenue and impact working with larger firms, I also don't want to add unnecessary complexity to my business and risk working with customers who don't get me and are a pain in the ass!

You know your perfect customer better than I do. It's your responsibility to make sure everyone on your team knows who they are and why you enjoy working with them.

Once you identify your perfect customer, the next step is to start selling, not only to validate your business model but also to maintain a constant feedback loop of the messaging, systems, and other processes that consistently close sales.

Now, it's important you ensure before you go to market you've taken the time to identify a market need where clients are already spending money. Regardless of how amazing an entrepreneur you think you are, and your grit and resilience to figure things out, if there is no market need, you will not be successful.

Whenever I hear of an entrepreneur who's been working on the same venture for six to seven years with little to no success, it solidifies in my mind they've failed to identify a market need. I'm not saying everyone is going to be an overnight success, but at some point you have to accept the reality of the situation. You either pivot by repositioning your company and value proposition, or you may need to start a new business altogether.

Trust me, as best as you can, you want to avoid swimming upstream in a market with limited demand, and if you're reading this book, more than likely you don't have enough time or money to do so. Instead, we want to focus on markets where prospects are already actively spending money and you know they have the problem your business is uniquely positioned to solve.

Once you've identified a market need and perfect customer, the next step is to look for opportunities and networks you're already a part of where you can solve that need for people you already know, like, and trust! This is key! Your first few customers will more than likely come from your network or someone within the vicinity of your network who can vouch for you.

If people are going to spend time with you, they need to trust you. If they don't know who you are, then it's unlikely they're going to trust you, unless you manage to borrow trust from someone else on your behalf.

I'm a personal fan of trying to find an auctioneer. This is someone in your immediate network willing to give you a chance and auction your services to their own company or the company they currently work for and are willing to risk their reputation to give you a try. You could spend the majority of your time focused on finding that auctioneer, if the juice is worth the squeeze.

I'm actively going through this process currently with IRONBOUND Boxing, looking for an auctioneer to help bring the IRONBOUND Courage Academy to life, our new facility in downtown Newark.

Once you get your initial foot in the door with an auctioneer, the next step is to get nine more. I interviewed marketing expert Asia Orangios, CEO of Demand Maven, who specializes at helping business-to-business (B2B) SaaS companies acquire their first hundred customers. I asked her during our interview how long it can take clients to get their first ten customers, and she stated, "It can be between six months to two years." Once again, please don't let that be you.

Sales can feel like hand-to-hand combat for the first hundred customers. During this time, your sales and marketing efforts should go side by side. Close the deal, deliver value to the client, then feature the client in a blog post, social media, or some other marketing asset in an effort to increase your trust and credibility and activate his or her network.

A great place to start is crafting your menu of products and services, along with a simple website or landing page. These two documents will set the foundation for your initial customer activation cycle. Your goal is to get potential customers moving along through your CAC, until they pay for your products and services and hopefully become raving fans.

In an ideal world, you come across a potential customer either online or at a networking event. If there is a warm prospect, you sell to them on the spot or send them to your website to kick off your CAC. If you sell services like me, the goal should be to get them on a call or an in-person meeting.

When I first started my entrepreneur journey, I didn't know the first thing about closing a client. I didn't have a customer activation cycle or menu of products and services, let alone a strong market demand. I read everything I could find on the internet and listened to multiple podcasts, but when it came time to take my idea to market, it was a bust. That's until I learned the framework and mindset you need to adopt in order to effectively close your first ten customers and, eventually, you're first one hundred.

I thought teaching corporate boxing to companies was a good idea, but in reality there wasn't a strong market pull, and I didn't approach the venture with the mindset of a salesman.

After launching IRONBOUND Media in June of 2020, I didn't go public with the venture initially. I closed my first three beta customers, initial clients to test the business model with, then transitioned away from corporate boxing to producing podcasts full-time. One of my business coach's frustrations with me previously was my reluctance to focus on sales, as if I thought they were magically going to happen. Before the pandemic when I was traveling to teach boxing classes in NYC, attempting to stand up IRONBOUND Boxing's for-profit arm, my business coach, Bill Watkins, frequently sent me audio text messages:

"Hey bro, it's your favorite man out in Jackson Hole, Wyoming. I want to know, all that shit you see on the internet is all bullshit. You need to get out there and make some sales, do whatever it is you got to do. Slick your hair back, comb your beard, and go close some deals. Over and out."

His advice didn't click with me until I launched IRONBOUND Media. I had a little experience under my belt by this point and knew what hadn't worked in the past, so when it came time to launch my new venture, I decided to do a complete 180 and do the exact opposite of what I did before, focusing on sales instead of hype to drive revenue.

After trying and failing to close incubators and accelerators, talking with a couple of executive directors and venture capitalists who were interested in podcasting but couldn't afford my price point, I decided to read between the lines and think about where I had a competitive advantage, or in military terms what I like to call tactical advantage. I realized out of my first three clients, two were veteran-owned businesses and organizations. As someone who had made a name for myself in the veteran community and enjoyed being around other veteran entrepreneurs, it dawned on me that's the market I should go after. My business coach group, The Lions Pride, catered to service academy graduates running small businesses, and I was already plugged in with Bunker Labs. I knew where veteran entrepreneurs hung out, what groups they were a part of, and how to contact them. Since I was charging a premium price point for my podcasts services, I knew I needed to target growth stage veteran-owned businesses, upward of a million plus in revenue, who could afford my premium services.

I created a quick three-step sales process: my initial customer activation cycle, which included onboarding clients with a thirty-minute consultation, followed by a one-hour working session to develop their tentative show, and then have them select a package at one of my three price points. From there I tapped my network and began inquiring if there was anyone interested in launching a podcast or curious about learning more. I learned my perfect customers weren't spending money on podcasts per se, but they were spending money on marketing and branding. I sensed a frustration amongst veteran entrepreneurs about the poor return on investment they were getting from their marketing and branding efforts and realized there was a golden opportunity for me to "dam the demand."

In The Lions Pride Slack channel, I engaged in multiple threads with veteran-owned business owners frustrated by the ROI they received from outsourced marketing and public relation agencies.

In his newsletter, *Category Pirates*, my friend and mentor Christopher Lochhead describes "dam the demand" as a business strategy that involves interrupting customers when they are shopping and educating them on the advantages of heading in a new and different direction ("You think you *want that*, but you really *need this!*). He goes on to say, "When you *dam* the demand, you're moving buyers in the category *from* the old *to* the new."

In my case, that meant moving veteran-owned small business owners away from relying on social media managers and ads for the brunt of their marketing and branding efforts to creating badass branded podcasts to engage their ideal audience.

I realized that since podcasting was not yet synonymous with brand building and a viable alternative to traditional marketing spend, I decided to create a new category called Dog Whistle Branding, encouraging veteran-owned businesses to treat their brands like dog whistles with the intention of only communicating with their perfect customers. IRONBOUND Media's podcast would be the whistles they'd need to blow on in order to communicate with them. I closed one of my first clients when I conveyed that we approached podcasting differently from other podcast agencies, encouraging our clients to start with a limited-edition ten-episode series, which was less daunting than thinking about releasing a show week over week.

Having a start and finish seemed more feasible to them, which I described as PLAPA, short for "podcasting like a platinum album." A platinum album is good ten, twenty, even thirty years later. Why not a podcast? When I used the phrase PLAPA, the client responded he had never thought of podcasting in that way and was sold on the idea. When I conveyed this message to Bill via text, he responded with the following message.

"Mmmmhmmm, Dog Whistle Branding."

As I thought about it later, I realized Dog Whistle Branding was the perfect positioning for IRONBOUND Media to be thought of as more than just another podcast agency. We were a category of one.

I updated my social media descriptions and started posting about Dog Whistle Branding. Every time I came across a potential prospect, I discussed our approach and philosophy. Before I knew it, I had a full pipeline of prospects and clients, primarily veterans, forcing me to scale up from a company of one to a company of five. I waited until I acquired ten customers before launching my own Dog Whistle Branding podcasts to drive leads for the business and generate more awareness. Until then, I focused purely on sales and showcasing the work we did for our clients.

I'm still working my way up to my first hundred, but in the meantime, I understand the importance of maintaining a sales mindset, supported by a strong CAC, and through understanding my perfect customer. As you go to market, throw away any reluctance you have to sales or recruit someone else who can sell. Otherwise, you will have a hard time getting your venture off the ground.

HOW THIS APPLIES TO YOU:
- Create a list of your first ten potential customers.
- Conduct direct one-on-one reach out to each one.
- Refine your brand's messaging based on what's working and what's not working.
- Deliver value.
- Capture testimonials and activate a referral network.

ADDITIONAL RESOURCES:

READ
- *This Is Marketing: You Can't Be Seen Until You Learn to See* by Seth Godin

- "1,000 True Fans? Try 100" by Li Jin, featured in A16Z Future

LISTEN

- *The Transition Podcast*: "How to Acquire Your First 100 Customers"
- *The Transition Podcast*: "How to Successfully Navigate Your First Go-To Market Journey," with Asian Orangios, CEO of Demand Maven

11

DEVELOP YOUR FLYWHEEL

"No matter how dramatic the end result, good-to-great transformations never happen in one fell swoop. In building a great company or social sector enterprise, there is no single defining action, no grand program, no one killer innovation, no solitary lucky break, no miracle moment. Rather, the process resembles relentlessly pushing a giant, heavy flywheel, turn upon turn, building momentum until a point of breakthrough, and beyond."

—JIM COLLINS, AUTHOR OF GOOD TO GREAT

You can't merely will your business into being successful. Maybe that happens in the movies or in magazine articles, but here in the real world, we achieve success through consistent actions.

Jim Collins is one of my all-time favorite business authors. Honestly, he and his books are one of the reasons I chose to write this book in the first place. I credit his *Good to Great* book series with empowering me with much of the business acumen I have today, in addition with the tutelage of my own business coach, Bill Watkins.

One of the business concepts he is best known for is the flywheel. I first learned about it while reading *Good to Great: Why Some Companies Make the Leap... and Others Don't*. Collins was the first to articulate that starting a venture is the equivalent of turning a giant heavy flywheel. At first, it feels like you are fighting against gravity. As you gradually start to turn the flywheel, you develop momentum, which you can build upon to accelerate. The more turns of the flywheel, the faster your acceleration.

The flywheel represents your underlying business architecture, one that leverages innovation to drive growth and ensures your venture survives the test of time.

BLACK SANDS ENTERTAINMENT

Army veteran Manuel Godoy and his wife, Geisel, started their own company, Black Sands Entertainment (BSE), together in 2015. What initially started as a self-funded video game company eventually developed into a publishing house for Black themed comic books that tell the history of Black people before slavery.

"We tell stories that Hollywood refuses to do, and we give the power to the fans."

Whether intentional or not, Manuel and Geisel built a hell of an underlying flywheel for BSE, leveraging storytelling, crowdfunding, and raving fans, allowing them to build a world-class independent comic book publishing house. Like most BVEs, the couple struggled to secure outside capital from traditional investors, including angels, venture capitalists, and banks. They knew they needed to look for alternative forms of funding.

In 2012, President Barack Obama signed into law the Jump Start Our Startups Act, more commonly known as the JOBS Act. The JOBS Act allows non-accredited investors to invest in early-stage start-ups, paving the way for crowdfunding.

After spending all of their money to build a demo for their first video game, *Kids 2 Kings*, they used crowdfunding to facilitate the pivot of the series into their first comic book. In 2017, they launched their first crowdfund on Kickstarter, securing $20,000 in funding to build their first comic book.

Despite having no formal background in comic book production, Manuel leveraged his passion for anime, short for Japanese animation, and writing to develop his own characters for BSE. Manuel began writing short stories at an early age, building up a skillset that translated perfectly to BSE's new direction. BSE's first comic book series was an instant hit, generating over $30,000 in revenue for the company and validating their new business model.

After still being unable to raise capital from traditional sources, including comic book publishers who didn't understand or appreciate the value of Black themed comic books, they returned to crowdfunding.

I was rejected multiple times by publishers in the industry after I sold over 25,000 comic books. So even though I had sold a lot of books, surpassing most expectations for an independent creator, we still couldn't get support.

Between 2017 and 2020, BSE successfully executed five crowdfunding campaigns, securing well over a $1 million to turn their company into the number one Black-owned publishing house in the country. They raised $500,000 from equity crowdfunding and generated over $1.2 million in revenue. Even with their impressive numbers, the company still couldn't raise capital traditionally.

You can't really believe the rumors if people don't even have the numbers to back up being a credible business. So when I was there and I finally had serious numbers, and I still was getting the rejections, I was like, "The game's rigged," right? And I can credibly say that. You can't tell me that I'm just imagining things.

From 2017 to 2022, BSE's consisted of the following:
- Create a comic book series that highlights the history of Black people before slavery.
- Invite readers to bring the series to life via equity crowdfunding.
- Produce a world-class comic book series.
- Distribute the series to raving fans.
- Generate revenue to produce a follow-on series.

In January of 2022, the hit television series *Shark Tank* invited BSE to pitch the company on the show. The team successfully walked away with a $500,000 commitment to invest from Mark Cuban and guest shark Kevin Hart.

They credit the success to their leadership and the company's flywheel for getting them to this point. With the wind at their back, Manuel and his team are on a mission to turn Black Sands Entertainment into a billion dollar publishing house, leveraging comic books, animation series, and other forms of intellectual property.

THE ELEMENTS OF A FLYWHEEL

A strong flywheel consists of the following key elements:
- Identify five to six core components of your business.
- Identify where your flywheel starts, i.e., the top of the loop, and what your company does above all else. It should be recession and pandemic proof and the key element that fuels your growth.
- Focus on the top of the flywheel.
- Identify the next four to five steps in the process and ensure each builds off one another, with an explanation of each.
- Outline a clear path back to the top of the loop.
- Be able to explain to internal and external stakeholders how your flywheel works and how to accelerate it.

Businesses don't always move as quickly as we would like.

It takes time for them to generate momentum, even after going through all the processes covered in the previous chapter. However, once you know how to develop your flywheel, you'll have a better understanding of where you should focus your efforts in order to drive momentum and accelerate growth. A strong flywheel will allow you to build a company that survives a recession, pandemic, or anything else life throws at you.

Success is compounded over time, and it's what you do consistently that increases the momentum of your flywheel.

The more it turns, the more growth you'll achieve.

IDENTIFY THE FIVE TO SIX CORE COMPONENTS OF YOUR BUSINESS

Start by taking a bird's eye view of your business and the underlying systems that run it. In every business, there are core components that define what you do.

For example, you come up with the idea to start a chocolate company that produces high-quality and sugar-free chocolate bars for healthy individuals who have a craving for sweets but don't want all the negative side effects of sugar.

For this business to work, not only do you have to identify premium ingredients to produce the chocolate, you also need to think about how to manufacture and distribute your product, maintain brand awareness and loyalty, and above all else, stay in business, regardless of any and all uncertainty.

Based on this example, let's breakdown the core components:

- Identify multiple high quality and natural cocoa farmers (pandemic proof/recession proof).
- Manufacture sugar-free chocolate bars for people who crave sweets and do not want the negative side effects (perfect customer).
- Distribute the product in markets and stores that the perfect customer frequents (distribution).
- Build brand loyalty and awareness through customers who opt for monthly subscriptions.
- Customers become brand evangelists, which rallies more people to purchase the product.
- Start back at the beginning.

In this example, you can see how to map the core components of your business. You can visualize them, knowing what your next step will be to keep the flywheel moving.

FOCUS ON THE TOP OF THE FLYWHEEL

Now that you know the core components of your business, the next step to get the flywheel moving is to focus on the most important tasks: identifying high quality and naturally sourced ingredients for the chocolate bars. As a brand, you are promising your customers that you produce a quality product. If you are unable to deliver on this brand promise, you have no reason to exist, which is why ingredients represent the top of your flywheel.

Regardless of rain, sleet, hail, or snow, or whether or not you have a pot to piss in, when it comes to the company above, the business is built around sourcing high quality ingredients.

At IRONBOUND Boxing, the top of our flywheel is "Focus on the impact." When things started to get rough during the pandemic and our gym was closed down, I had to remind myself that we could still serve the community. We could still make an impact. A gym was a nice-to-have, not a necessity, and IRONBOUND Boxing has always been about more than boxing. Although we couldn't train inside our gym, we could still do socially distanced workouts in the park. Our team of volunteers began mobilizing workouts at the park, and we got back in the fight.

At IRONBOUND Media, the top of my flywheel is establishing our company as an authority on marketing, branding, and category design for veteran-owned businesses. Although we focus on podcasts production currently, that's not to say we will only do that in the future. We're focused on clock building, not time telling.

Jim Collins masterfully wrote in his book, *Built to Last: Successful Habits of Visionary Companies*, "Having a great idea or being a charismatic visionary leader is 'time telling'; building a company that can prosper far beyond the tenure of any single leader and through multiple product life cycles is 'clock building.' Those who build visionary companies tend to be clock builders. Their primary accomplishment is not the implementation of a great idea, the expression of a charismatic personality, or the accumulation of wealth. It is the company itself and what it stands for."

Searching for a single great idea and basing your success on it is time telling; building a process to generate 1,000 great ideas is clock building. The top of your flywheel needs to be clock building, not time telling.

IDENTIFY THE NEXT FOUR TO FIVE STEPS IN THE PROCESS AND ENSURE EACH BUILDS OFF ONE ANOTHER

The only way the flywheel works is when there is consistent momentum. The process has to be interconnected; otherwise, you'll throw off your flywheel.

For the chocolate company, it's a natural flow to go from producing the chocolate bars to distributing them. Obviously there's a lot of small steps in-between, such as packaging the bars, shipping them to the distributor, and so on. But when it comes to your flywheel, you don't want to focus on the tedious details, only the core components.

It wouldn't make sense for us to build brand loyalty and awareness before distributing the product and getting it in the hands of the perfect customer.

If you're having trouble, you can start by reverse engineering the process and working your way around the flywheel in the opposite direction by asking, "What did it take for us to continue sourcing high quality ingredients? We need cash to pay the farmers, which is generated by selling our product, made possible by strong brand awareness. To meet consumer demand, we need to get the product in customers' hands, which is made possible by a strong distribution network."

OUTLINE A CLEAR PATH BACK TO THE TOP OF THE LOOP

To keep the flywheel spinning, there must be a clear path back to the top of the loop. Based on our example above, the more brand evangelists and customers we have, the more revenue we're able to generate, enabling us to continue purchasing high quality ingredients.

BE ABLE TO EXPLAIN TO INTERNAL AND EXTERNAL STAKEHOLDERS HOW YOUR FLYWHEEL WORKS AND HOW TO ACCELERATE IT

Not everyone you come across is going to be well-versed in the flywheel concept, particularly your internal stakeholders, such as your staff. However, it's important to understand the overall architecture of your business and how it works together. The simplest way to do this is to create a visual flywheel and share it with your team.

Even if you're a solo founder, the flywheel will give you a better understanding of how your company works and where to focus your efforts when it comes to growth.

YOUR FLYWHEEL ISN'T YOUR SALES CYCLE

One of the mistakes I made early on was confusing my sales cycle with my business flywheel. In order to generate momentum for IRONBOUND Media, I create free educational content to build brand awareness amongst veteran-owned business owners. When I mapped out my first flywheel, I built it around the specific activities to drive revenue, specifically podcasting, instead of the underlying business architecture. In other words, I was still trying to tell time.

Your flywheel isn't your step-by-step process to close a point of sale. It's your process as a company to deliver value in the market.

Visit www.BlackVeteranEntrepreneurs.com/Flywheel to download your worksheet to develop your flywheel.

HOW THIS APPLIES TO YOU:
- Develop a flywheel for your business model.
- Make sure each stage builds upon the next.
- Share the flywheel with internal stakeholders (staff, board members, and anyone else).

ADDITIONAL RESOURCES:

READ
- *Good to Great: Why Some Companies Make the Leap… and Others Don't* by Jim Collins
- *Turning the Flywheel: A Monograph to Accompany Good to Great* by Jim Collins

LISTEN
- *Dog Whistle Branding*: "What's Your Brand's Flywheel?"
- *The Knowledge Project*: "Keeping the Flywheel in Motion, featuring Jim Collins," episode 67

12

DON'T BE AFRAID TO FUND YOURSELF

"I had to make my own living and my own opportunity. But I made it! Don't sit down and wait for the opportunities to come. Get up and make them."

—MADAM C.J. WALKER

If there's one deterrent that prevents BVEs from pursuing their entrepreneurial ambitions, it's access to capital in order to cover their businesses initial start-up costs.

As BVEs, we need capital to purchase inventory, hire developers for our technology products, and cover other basic operating expenses. Without capital, the idea of being an entrepreneur can feel like a distant dream.

Just like the old saying goes "there's more than one way to skin a cat," the same rings true for funding your venture, regardless of the systemic issues that make it feel impossible. I'm here to tell you that regardless of your background and how daunting your venture may seem, there are ways to fund your business. Sometimes you just have to get creative and think outside of the box.

MUTT SAUCE

When Charlynda Scales came up with the idea to start a company in memory of her late grandfather, Charley "Mutt" Ferrel, Jr., she knew she needed start-up capital.

For the past several years, as an active duty Air Force officer, Charlynda had been saving money to purchase her dream car, a BMW. What may seem like a trivial goal to some was a big deal for someone who grew up in the projects.

You grow up being told you don't have a lot, and then when you finally get on active duty and get a steady paycheck, you can save money. So my dream was to walk into a BMW lot and pay cash for my car. That was my dream.

That all changed one day, nearly eight years after her grandfather passed away from cancer, when Charlyanda's mother handed her an envelope containing her grandfather's secret recipe, a staple of the family since 1956.

It was the only copy of the recipe, which he kept in his wallet.

When she asked her mom why he left her the recipe, her response was, "He just told me to give it to you."

After receiving the recipe, Charlynda had a dream one night.

Call it cliché, but I dreamt of walking into the little country store that sat on top of the hill where we lived. In the dream, there was nothing in the store except bottles of sauce. On every shelf. With his face on it. I woke up and opened my laptop.

Mutt Sauce was born.

To bring her vision to life, she knew she needed capital. So Charlynda made the tough decision to allocate the money she saved for her dream car to fund the business.

So I'm sitting there, like, I can have a BMW or I could have this business that I have no idea what's going to happen with it. It could fail. I could lose everything. People could hate it. 'Cause I haven't even tried it yet. I haven't even tried the sauce yet. So I just went ahead and did it. I paid for everything. I paid for the manufacturing, for the labels, everything that was involved in the start-up.

For the next five years, Charlynda continued to bootstrap the business, even after she left active duty, working different jobs to pay the bills and keep the lights on. Whatever it took to keep the dream alive.

Charlynda spent a year working full-time on Mutt Sauce before having to find employment due to the financial burden and stress it was causing in her life.

In 2017, she had her first big break after she won a $25,000 grant from Bob Evans Farm and an opportunity to receive mentorship from Daymond John, celebrity investor and founder of FUBU.

Under Daymond's mentorship, and with the money she received from Bob Evans, Charlynda used the funds to invest in hiring a new manufacturer to produce Mutt Sauce. The new manufacturer was closer to home, allowing her to increase production and meet the necessary requirements to get Mutt Sauce in Kroger grocery stores in Dayton, Ohio.

Today, Mutt Sauce is still going strong with the goal of reaching over six figures by the end of 2022. The pandemic caused its fair share of setbacks, forcing Charlynda to shift her business model to primarily e-commerce and essentially rebuilding her business from the ground up.

She recently had a son. He serves as extra motivation for her to build generation wealth and build Mutt Sauce into a nationally recognized brand.

NO EXCUSES

This might come across as harsh, but rather than coming up with reasons why you can't get capital to fund your business, channel that energy to come up with solutions.

The intent is not to discredit the reality that challenge Black founders, but to drive focus to what you *can* control. This means you may have to get scrappy and work a part-time job, maybe several, or launch a pre-sale in order to fund initial production.

Be solution driven, not only in creating your business idea but also in how you grow that business and how you approach all the obstacles you will face.

MY JOURNEY BOOTSTRAPPING

"I'm thinking of starting a new company, producing branded podcasts for businesses," I told my coaching group at The Lions Pride during our quarterly tactical advance in September 2020.

The pandemic was kicking my butt, literally and figuratively. Teaching virtual boxing classes was not how I envisioned my future, and I needed a way out. I started teaching classes as a way to pay my bills since I wasn't taking a salary from a nonprofit.

The following weekend, I purchased a domain for IRONBOUND Media and created a website. Thankfully I had a lot of practice over the years, due to my bootstrapper mentality.

I already had podcast equipment for my show, *Confessions of a Native Son,* and figured I could use the same equipment to produce shows for clients.

My goal was to get profitable as soon as possible so I could keep my overhead low. I decided to continue teaching virtual boxing classes until I could replace the income I was making with IRONBOUND Media.

For the next three months, I hit the ground running. I tapped my network to let everyone know I was producing podcasts. I focused primarily on direct outreach instead of brand marketing.

I closed three clients in the fall of 2020, all of which I invoiced up front, giving me positive cash flow and allowing me to transition away from corporate into IRONBOUND Media full-time. I wasn't exactly printing money, but I no longer had to sweat on camera all day and could focus on scaling up my business.

I reinvested the profits back into my business, put myself on a meager salary, hired an audio engineer, and began to gradually scale up my team. Within my first year in business, I managed to generate over six figures in revenue, with the goal of reaching half a million in the next year or so.

What started out as a company of one is now a team of six contractors, producing shows and building brands for clients all across the country.

I'm still not printing money yet, but I'm having fun and continuing to grow.

WHAT ABOUT NONPROFITS?

Yes, you can bootstrap nonprofits too. In the early days, you are investing a lot of hours and manpower you are not being compensated for, and that's okay.

Start by focusing on one core program. This is going to be your bread and butter, setting the foundation for your organization to build upon. It can be a tutoring program, sports team, or in my case, a boxing gym.

Obviously you are going to need some funding to get things started, but you can circumvent a lot of the upfront cost through in-kind donations, a non-cash gift including goods, services, and expertise. Start by sending a thoughtful message to potential donors and supporters in your network, letting them know what you're working on and how they can support. In the early days of starting a nonprofit, it helps when you can be crystal clear about what you need.

Ninety-five percent of the IRONBOUND Boxing Academy's initial start-up cost were covered through in-kind donations, including gloves, equipment, and even our badass heavy bag structure. Thank you, Metropolitan Walters!

We did end up receiving approximately $10,000 in funding from the NYPD Boxing Team and some veterans within my personal network. The Boxing Academy was our flagship program, so we invested blood, sweat, and tears to bring it to life.

For nearly two years we operated on a limited budget of less than $10,000 a year. While it might not seem ideal for most, we still built a nationally recognized brand from the ground up. If I had to do it all over again, I'd do the same thing.

The idea of getting kids in the inner-city out of the street and into the gym resonates with people all across the country, especially veterans. My background as a Naval

Academy boxing champion and Marine officer and starting a free gym for Newark youth caught people's attention. I took photos and videos of kids training, sharing them on social media or at in-person events. I was IRONBOUND Boxing's chief evangelist, telling anyone who would listen why boxing changes lives.

The best thing you can do for your organization is tell the story and sell the vision. Use whatever means are available to get the word out. Be thoughtful and people understand your why.

I DIDN'T FORGET ABOUT STARTUPS

Some business models, particularly tech start-ups, do require a large upfront investment of capital to build the product and go to market. However, I firmly believe you can increase your chances of success by generating traction, validating the demand for what you're offering through sign ups, beta customers, etc..

Incubators and accelerators encourage start-up founders to build an MVP (minimum viable product), the most basic version of the product you can build on your own. You'd be surprised how far you can go with a solid MVP.

If that seems too daunting, I recommend you follow Sahil Lavingia's advice in *The Minimalist Entrepreneur* and replace "most valuable product" with "manual valuable process."

In the book, Sahil states, "Refine a manual valuable process before building a minimum viable product." This means in the early days, when you can't afford to build an app, solve your customers' problems the old fashion way without technology but instead with a step-by-step process.

For example, instead of building a social media app, maybe you organize an in-person meetup, leveraging email and existing social media channels to drive sign-ups.

It doesn't take much to get started. The key is starting!

You have to decide how serious you are about bringing your vision to life. I'm a big proponent of putting skin in the game, and while I've heard of founders using other people's money (OPM) to fund their businesses, this doesn't apply to the majority of BVEs I've come across.

OPM is a nice to have, not a necessity. So shift your mindset, get scrappy, and get to work.

HOW THIS APPLIES TO YOU:
- Create a list of the various different ways you can fund your business (part-time job, grants, etc.).
- Use the profits you're able to generate from selling products and services to reinvest back into your business.
- Keep your overhead low and scale up gradually.
- If you decide to launch a nonprofit, seek in-kind donations in addition to financial ones.
- Be resilient and understand that for bootstrappers, this is a marathon, not a sprint.

ADDITIONAL RESOURCES:

READ
- *The Minimalist Entrepreneur: How Great Founders Do More with Less* by Sahil Lavingia
- *Start Small, Stay Small: Developer's Guide to Launching a Startup* by Rob Walling

LISTEN
- *The Transition* podcasts: "Turning a family recipe into a bustling brand with Charlynda Scales, Founder and CEO of Mutt Sauce LLC"
- *Startups For the Rest of Us* hosted by Rob Walling

P.S. You'll notice in this chapter I left out specific finance information. I'm not a CPA or CFA, nor do I have a strong background in finance. There are people way more equipped than me who can provide great information on this topic, which I've listed below.

READ
- *Profit First: Transform Your Business from a Cashing Eating Monster to a Money-Making Machine* by Mike Michalowicz
- *How Finance Works: The HBR Guide to Thinking Smart About The Numbers* by Mihir Desai
- *Financial Management: The Ultimate Guide to Planning, Organizing, Directing, and Controlling the Financial Activities of an Enterprise* by Greg Shields

13

WHAT IT TAKES TO WIN

"The fight is won or lost far away from the witnesses, behind the lines, in the gym and out there on the road, long before I dance under those lights."

—MUHAMMAD ALI

Strategy and planning are one thing, but execution is an entirely different beast. To close the gap between the three, at some point you'll need to adopt a management system to get things done.

Trust me, I know what it's like to sit by yourself at home, or in a coworking space, with no idea how you're going to accomplish all the goals and aspirations you set for yourself. You have to build an operating or management system to run your business on.

Over the years, I've tried multiple management systems, from Gino Wickman's *Traction* framework, Sean Covey's *The 4 Disciplines of Execution*, and Verne Harnish's *Rockefeller Habits*, just to name a few. Of all the ones I've utilized thus far, I believe the two most beneficial to

BVEs, especially during the initial launch phase of your venture, is a combination of the "playing to win (PTW)" framework, outlined in the book, *Playing to Win: How Strategy Really Works*, by A.G. Lafley and Roger L. Martin, combined with the "objectives and key results (OKR)" framework, first appearing in print in John Doerr's book, *Measure What Matters: How Google, Bono, and the Gates Foundation Rock the World with OKRs*, and more recently the advice in *Radical Focus: Achieving Your Most Important Goals with Objectives and Key Results*, by Christina Wodtke.

When you're first starting out, you feel like you're making it up as you go, but taking the time to adopt a simple management system gets rid of those feelings. Suddenly, you know what result you want to achieve, you have a clear plan to get there, and you have a way to track your progress.

To win in business and achieve flawless acceleration by leveraging the OKR and PTW framework, you'll need to adopt the following steps:
1. Set your strategic plan.
2. Set annual and quarterly objectives to focus on.
3. Pick three key results that each objective will allow you to accomplish.
4. Set weekly priorities to drive results.
5. Measure your progress.

PLAYING TO WIN
Regardless of where you are in your venture, having a strategic plan will help accomplish your goals and

streamline your execution, especially as you grow from a team of one to a team of many.

A good strategic plan sets the vision for your company and gives you an asset to share with internal and external stakeholders. In my coaching group, The Lions Pride, we use a modified version of Verne Harnishe's one-page strategic plan, which we refer to as the one-page business plan, a single-page overview of a company's priorities, vision, and direction, including brand information, strengths and weaknesses, and the OKRs for the year and quarter.

A fully developed strategic plan can be a bit daunting in the early stages, so I believe you can benefit more by developing your initial strategy utilizing the playing to win framework below.

The book, *Playing to Win: How Strategy Really Works*, discusses the strategies utilized by Procter and Gamble, where A.G. Lafley served as chairman of the board and CEO for thirteen years, dominating the consumer goods industry. Roger Martin, dean of the University of Toronto's Rotman School of Management and one of the top management thinkers in the world, states, "The two most fundamental strategic choices are deciding where to play and how to win."

You execute strategy through the decisions you make on a daily basis, the market opportunity you choose to go after, and how you aim to succeed.

Martin's approach to strategy is summed up as follows:

- What is your winning aspiration? What are you hoping to accomplish?
- Where will you play? What market and industry are you aiming to dominate in order to win?
- How will you win? How will you bring your vision to life?
- What capabilities must be in place? What tools and resources do you need to win?
- What management systems are required? From a management and leadership perspective, what systems need to be in place?

What I like the most about this framework is it breaks strategy down into a clear and concise way. You don't need some fancy spreadsheet and PowerPoint® presentation to map it out, just a Google document or a scratch piece of paper.

There was a time in my life when I was intimidated by strategy, as if it was some magical skill learned at elite business schools and management consulting firms. But for those of us in the trenches of our ventures, the PTW framework helps explain our vision and how we plan to get there.

As you scale up from one-of-one to a team of many, you have to constantly communicate your strategy to your team so they understand the "why" behind the decisions and choices you make.

Once you answer the following questions, the next step is to set annual and quarterly objectives to bring your vision to life, as outlined in Christina Wodtke's book, *Radical Focus.*

RADICAL FOCUS

In the fall of 2020, I had an opportunity to hear Wodtke speak at a Tactical Advance event with The Lions Pride, our quarterly planning events. Although at the time I was familiar with the OKR process, I didn't have a thorough understanding of the framework.

During her talk, Wodtke emphasized the importance of keeping things simple by focusing on one to two key objectives that will result in the biggest outcome rather than amassing a giant to-do list for our teams.

For the past few years, I failed to keep things simple, often mapping out loft and ambitious goals for IRONBOUND Boxing, ranging from launching new programs, building a new gym, and so much more. I'd leave a quarterly planning session with clarity and focus, feeling energized for what lies ahead, but after a few weeks back in the grind, I kept adding more and more to my plate until my original goals were sidetracked. As a result, I'd get to the end of the quarter and realize I didn't accomplish what I set out to do.

I learned from Wodtke that this was common, and in order to mitigate it, she recommended we limit our number of quarterly objectives, set up a weekly cadence of tracking and accountability, and be relentless about executing.

Wodtke taught the OKR process at the highest levels of Silicon Valley and at conferences all across the globe. She's witnessed flawless acceleration in action, and after hearing her talk and reading her book, I decided to fully commit to adopting the process at all things IRONBOUND.

At any given time, there are multiple and often conflicting responsibilities that come with running a venture. However, in order to move forward and build a company that can operate like a well-oiled machine, you have to learn how to set goals and execute on them.

In any business, there's a core set of activities and actions that drive the majority of the results. This belief is commonly referred to as the "Pareto Principle," which asserts that 80 percent of results are driven by 20 percent of effort.

Before setting your objective, first identify the top priorities that drive the majority of the results, then quantify the information to your team in your team's objective, both annually and quarterly.

Once you do, whether you're a solo founder or have a team to support, focus on accomplishing your objective.

For example, let's say you plan on opening a restaurant or barber shop. There's a lot that goes into the process, such as finding a building, securing funding, and countless other steps. However, before you can think about opening, you might want to start by creating a simplified business plan to get your thoughts out of your head and on paper.

In that case, the objective would be conveyed as the following: "Create a simplified business plan for the barbershop."

Let's say you're a nonprofit organization, similar to IRONBOUND Boxing, and you want to launch a financial literacy program at your local community center. To get started, you need to secure funding from an anchor donor to cover the costs of the program. In that case, a good objective would be: "Secure anchor donors to help cover financial costs of our upcoming financial literacy program."

The clearer you can make the objective, the easier it will be to convey not only to yourself, but to internal and external team members, such as vendors and advisors, as well.

Whatever objective you choose, make sure it drives momentum in your business. For first-time BVEs, your sole focus should be on validating your business model, i.e., verifying you've identified a problem and customers are willing to pay you to solve it. This will pay off dividends in the long run—trust me.

KEY RESULTS

After identifying your annual and quarterly objectives, the next item in the process is to determine what accomplishing them will allow your company to do.

According to Christina Wodtke, "A key result is a metric that quantifies your objective. The Objective is aspirational and uses inspiring language, which is often vague. The key result makes that inspiring language specific." In the words of Malcolm X, "Make it plain." Leave nothing to speculation. You want to identify exactly what results you're going for.

In the example above regarding financial literacy, as a result of securing an anchor donor, you'll be able to launch a pilot program.

A good result would be: "Successfully launch a pilot program within three to six months."

Another key result can be tied to the number of kids or young adults you can impact through the program. A second key result could be: "Successfully train thirty to fifty kids in our financial literacy curriculum."

The final key result could potentially be: "Secure follow-on funding to allow the program to continue."

For every objective, list no more than three key results.

SET YOUR PRIORITIES FOR THE WEEK

In his book, *Deep Work*, Cal Newport discussed the concept of lead and lag measures to describe the set of consistent actions that result in the desired outcomes. Newport explains that lag measures are the goals you're ultimately trying to accomplish, while lead measures are the behaviors that allow you to do so.

The easiest way to understand this concept is to think about running a marathon. If you've never ran before, the idea of running 26.2 miles straight can seem daunting and overwhelming. However, instead of focusing on the entire mileage, committing to running twenty to thirty minutes a day, for two to three months, seems a lot more doable. If you can do so, then you'll be more than prepared to successfully complete your first marathon.

The same concept applies when setting and accomplishing goals for your business.

Identify the sets of behaviors that will produce the desired results. If you need to write a business plan, the lead measure would be blocking off a set amount of time each week to work on it.

If you find yourself in a cash crunch and need to generate revenue as soon as possible, your lead measure could be calling and talking with five to ten potential customers a day. It's all about identifying the actions you can control and executing on them on a daily, weekly, and monthly basis.

WHAT'S SO SPECIAL ABOUT OKRS?
For several years, I've struggled with goal setting in my ventures—until I adopted the OKR process I first read about in *Radical Focus*. After reading the book from end to end over the course of two days, I taught myself how to map out the OKR process on a blank sheet of paper.

I also began adopting the OKR process in IRONBOUND Boxing and IRONBOUND Media. One of my issues has always been around execution. When running a non-profit, I get pulled in multiple directions, between managing programs, fundraising, and coaching at the gym.

I knew to get us to the next level, I had to do something different, and I decided to implement the OKR process. I've found it's a lot easier to rally my team around one goal instead of multiple ones.

I decided to do the same thing with IRONBOUND Media.

In the Fall of 2020, I decided to launch the *Dog Whistle Branding (DWB)* podcast for IRONBOUND Media. The purpose of the podcast was to position us as an authority around marketing and branding, while evangelizing the DWB category.

I sketched out the plan for the show in Google Docs, and once I learned the objective and key results process, I decided to make the show's launch the objective for the quarter.

My goal was to launch the *DWB* podcast and make it the number one lead magnet for IRONBOUND Media. In order to accomplish this, I planned to record ten to fifteen veteran-owned business owners, release an episode a week, and begin building an audience around the show.

I started recording a few months prior to the live event but was dragging my feet on releasing it due to other obligations. Once I committed to it as my objective and key results, I drew up a white board and placed it behind my desk. Every day I walked into my podcasts studio, I saw the objective on the board.

It wasn't until a few weeks into the quarter, I looked up at the board and realized I was failing at it. Not only had I not launched the podcast, I was acting as if it was not even a focus of mine. Running multiple ventures has a way of doing that.

Thankfully, having to stare my inactivity in the face every day forced me to focus and get it done.

Rather than making excuses, I committed to the launch date for the show, officially releasing it two weeks later. Sure enough, not only did I successfully release the show, I also met my Q4 revenue goal.

Below is the following framework for the OKR process.

Objective: (This is where you place your one goal for the quarter. This should be a goal to inspire and rally your team around.)

Key results allow you to measure the chances of success for accomplishing your goal. If you accomplish your objective, list what the expected results will be.

Key result 1
Key result 2
Key result 3

Each week, you and your team need to set priorities for what to focus on. List no more than three priorities.

Priorities 1
Priorities 2
Priorities 3

DO NOT FORGET ABOUT THE LEAD MEASURES
Something I'm always cognizant of with goal setting are lead and lag measures, which I first read in Cal Newport's book, *Deep Work*. Lag measures inform us whether or not we accomplished our goals. Lead measures are the actions we take on a consistent daily, weekly, and monthly basis that put us in the best position to accomplish them.

Like many of you, I'm guilty of focusing too much on accomplishing goals rather than consistent actions to accomplish them.

For instance, when it came to writing this book, I was excited for the opportunity to be an author and publish my first book, but I felt overwhelmed by how much work had to get done.

Rather than allowing that to get to me, I decided to focus on what I had immediate control over: writing. I realized as long as I write every day, I'm confident I can obtain the necessary word count for a book.

Although I didn't write every day, whenever I felt over-whelmed, rather than stress or think about it, I focused on writing.

I'd argue that for early stage BVEs earning $50,000 or less in their venture, your first OKR should be around validating the business model or driving revenue. A good example of an OKR would be "Identify and validate your perfect customer." This will rally your team to niche down and focus on the key activity to drive the best result.

If you're a product-based business, such as an apparel company, your OKR could be around creating your first addition of apparel or swag. If you're planning on opening a brick and mortar gym or restaurant, your OKR can be around finding a location and securing a lease.

It's hard enough to focus on one OKR without bouncing around all over the place, so stay focused.

Example of IRONBOUND Media's strategic plan 2022:

WINNING ASPIRATION:
1. Establish IRONBOUND Media as the premiere brand strategy and positioning firm for veteran-owned businesses.
   a. Leverage audio, strategy, and content creation to help brands stand out from the crowd, channel through the noise, and engage with their perfect customer.

WHERE WILL WE PLAY?
1. Brand strategy and positioning for early and growth stage veteran-owned businesses

2. Podcast production

3. Category design

HOW WILL WE WIN?

1. Establish IRONBOUND Media as the category king of *Dog Whistle Branding*. We build trust in authority by getting badass results for all our clients and teaching what we know via the following mediums:
   a. Podcasts
   b. Newsletters
   c. Blogs

WHAT CAPABILITIES MUST BE IN PLACE?

1. Ability to manage and work with multiple brands

2. Trust and authority in the veteran ecosystem

WHAT MANAGEMENT SYSTEMS ARE REQUIRED?

1. Company operating system

2. Customer resource management system

3. Badass content production process

QUARTERLY OBJECTIVES

Objective: Build and implement a badass seven-step content production plan.

Key results 1: Have all content edited and uploaded five to seven days prior to its release.

Key results 2: Successfully run and operate three to five IRONBOUND Media shows.

Key results 3: Stress free is the way to be!

Priority 1: Schedule a one-hour content planning session with team.

Priority 2: Finalize *The Transition* and *Dog Whistle Branding* content calendar.

Priority 3: Schedule production calls with all our clients.

Upcoming projects: *BVE* book release October 2022

HOW THIS APPLIES TO YOU:
- Build your company's strategic plan utilizing the *Playing to Win* framework.
- Set objectives and key results each quarter.
- Track your progress.

ADDITIONAL RESOURCES:

READ
- *Playing To Win: Playing to Win: How Strategy Really Works* by Roger L. Martin and A.G. Lafley
- *Radical Focus: Achieving Your Most Important Goals with Objectives and Key Results* by Christina Wodtke

LISTEN
- *The Transition Podcast*: "Radical Focus: Achieving Your Most Important Goals with Objectives and Key Results, with author Christina Wodtke"
- *Dog Whistle Branding*: "Playing to Win"

14

FOCUS IS KEY

"It's not about what you're capable of, it's about what you're willing to do."

—MIKE TOMLIN, HEAD COACH OF
THE PITTSBURGH STEALERS

At this point, I've given you all the tools and frameworks to successfully launch a venture, but it is on you to stay focused, committed, and execute.

When I was in high school, my basketball coaches, John Reese and Chris Jones, came up with the saying "Focus 32." High school basketball games consist of eight-minute quarters, and the term "Focus 32" meant complete concentration for eight minutes, each quarter, in order to win.

I graduated high school in 2005, and almost eighteen years later, the term still sticks with me. While your business isn't a basketball game, the principle still applies. If you want to succeed, you have to focus.

IF YOU DON'T PRIORITIZE IT, IT WON'T HAPPEN

Think back to October 2016, when I first began working on the IRONBOUND Boxing Academy. At the time, I was a graduate student, working a full-time job, and spending all my free time bringing the vision to life. It was overwhelming, to be frank. Although my partners and I got it done, we didn't have all the tools and frameworks I shared with you in this book. We just went off our gut.

Now that you do have all these tools and a framework, you are lightyears ahead of me when I began.

Focusing is something I still struggle with. I'm a visionary, and oftentimes I get distracted by shiny objects, whether that's launching a new podcast series, starting a new program for IRONBOUND Boxing, or coming up with new business models all together. But when I think about the greatest successes I've had in life, they've all come through intense focus.

Even now, when I think back to October 2016, I was just a guy with an idea for a free gym. I didn't have much money or any friends or family in the area, just a relentless focus and determination to build a gym. At the time I was attending graduate school, working full-time, and building a nonprofit from the ground. I say all this to say I know how difficult and overwhelming life can be, but when you set a goal and focus on accomplishing it, you can move mountains.

Can you give your idea your undivided focus every minute of every day? No. And that's not what I am asking you to do. What I am saying is when you can give it time, give it all of your focus in the moment. Whether that is ten minutes or ten hours, focus.

Just chip away at it bit by bit. One of my favorite sayings is "Kaizen," a Japanese phrase for small incremental improvements over time. When you're just starting out, it may be difficult to see progress in your venture when you don't have clients or customers and feel like you're spinning on a hamster wheel. But as long as you show up and do the work, utilizing the frameworks in each chapter, you will make progress. I promise you.

My hope is that by following the frameworks outlined in each chapter, you have everything you need to get started and succeed.

15

ALWAYS BE LEARNING

"People don't realize how a man's whole life can be changed by one book."

—MALCOLM X

There's never been a better time to be an entrepreneur. Thanks to the internet and the access it provides to entrepreneurial education, the path is wide open for you.

Between podcasts, online workshops, and access to various education programs, including accelerators and incubators, with the right mindset, you can learn almost anything, even podcasting!

In September 2019, as a part-time contractor with WeWork focused on veteran entrepreneurship, I helped organize a series of podcast interviews for a limited-series entitled "Find Your Mission." The series' intent was to feature interviews with military veterans and share their entrepreneurial journey.

Although I recommended entrepreneurs to interview, the actual production was handled by an award winning podcast agency called Mission.org. Mission and WeWork conducted a total of twelve interviews, including one with yours truly.

Although I had done multiple podcast interviews at this point, I never worked with an actual production company. When I showed up at the WeWork office on West 35th Street in New York City where the interviews were being conducted, I met the Mission producer, Hilary, at the front desk. Expecting her to arrive with a large set-up, to my surprise, I noticed all she had with her was a baseball cap and a backpack. I immediately greeted her and headed up the stairs to conduct our interview.

When we got into the office, she opened up her backpack and pulled out a laptop, a microphone, and a mobile podcast mixer the size of a hand.

Shocked, I said, "That's your podcast set up?"

"Yep! That's it."

I knew I was in the wrong business at that exact moment! From then on, I knew I wanted to start a business in podcasting. I had no idea how to produce a show, but I was bound to figure it out.

Once I finished the interview, I asked Hillary to email me her gear equipment, and she kindly obliged. Later that week when I received her email, I immediately purchased the equipment online, along with multiple audiobooks on podcasting.

From the time I conducted the Mission.org interview in September 2019 up until I launched my first podcast, *Confessions of a Native Son*, in February of 2020, I read five books on podcasting, watched countless YouTube videos, and began networking with podcasters in NYC.

Although the pandemic gave me a nudge to pull the trigger and eventually build my own podcast production company, Mission.org had already planted the seed.

Prior to my interview, I didn't know the first thing about producing podcasts, but I didn't let that stop me. I took advantage of the internet and taught myself. The internet has opened up a world of possibilities for the education of BVEs unlike ever before, but it's on us to take advantage of it.

I'm not the only BVE who has adopted this mindset.

HAMPDEN FARMS

In 2016, Air Force veteran Zephrine Hansen and her husband relocated from California to Denver, Colorado, to find space to raise their three autistic children. The following year she participated in a life changing therapeutic horticulture farm program for veterans focused on wellness and mental health called Veterans to Farmers.

The experience sparked her interest in the farming and agricultural movement. Shortly after completing the program, Zephrine started Hampden Farms, a suburban farming project offering sustainable farming solutions and small-batch artisanal products made from organic ingredients, lovingly grown and conscientiously sourced.

"Farming saved my life and then gave me everything I ever wanted emotionally, spiritually, and physically, opening opportunities I never imagined."

For years, Zephrine made homemade lotion and wellness products for her three young children, each of whom are autistic and suffer from eczema. Once she became exposed to the agricultural community, she realized she could grow her own ingredients for her products, along with other makers in her community.

Zephrine started reading books on farming, including *Farming While Black: Soul Fire Farm's Practical Guide to Liberation on the Land* by Leah Penniman, as well as business books by Carla A. Harris.

She also began seeking out entrepreneurial and agricultural programs to teach her how to build a sustainable farming business. Nowadays, Zephrine describes herself as an "agripreneur," despite having no formal background in farming and agriculture prior to starting Hampden.

KNOWLEDGE IS EVERYWHERE. YOU HAVE TO SEEK IT OUT.

Start with the mindset that no one is going to save you or your business, so it's on you to take a proactive approach to learning, whether it's reading books, attending workshops, or scouring the internet for educational content. The world is a giant university, and now thanks to the internet, it's at your fingertips.

Venture capitalist and modern philosopher Naval Ravikant states in an unpublished bonus section of Eric Jorgensen's book, *The Almanack of Naval Ravikant: A Guide to Wealth and Happiness*, "Now we have the internet, which is the greatest weapon of knowledge ever created, completely interconnected. It's very easy to learn. The ability to learn, the means of learning, the tools of learning, are abundant and infinite. It's the desire that's incredibly scarce."

The internet provides BVEs with access to professors and mentors, including some of the most prolific minds in business, including Booker T. Washington, Jim Collins, and more recently Naval Ravikant. It doesn't matter whether or not you get to meet them in person. You can learn from them through books, blogs, podcasts, and more recently, YouTube University.

There used to be no such thing as self-guided learning. Now, if you actually have the desire to learn, everything is on the internet. You can go on Khan Academy. You can get MIT and Yale lectures online. You can get all the coursework and interactivity. You can read blogs by brilliant people. You can read all these great books.

The only reason I know about Naval is through the recommendation of a fellow Marine and venture capitalist who told me to listen to his podcasts, *How to Get Rich (Without Getting Lucky)*. He gave the recommendation, I took action and listened.

Personally, I'm an autodidact. I learn all day every day, rotating between books, podcasts, and YouTube. I was never a good student in school, but once I decided to launch IRONBOUND Boxing, I knew I had to figure stuff out on my own, which awakened a thirst for knowledge inside me I never knew existed.

Truth be told, due to my subpar academic performance in high school and college, I always thought I wasn't very smart, despite graduating from such a prestigious college as the Naval Academy and eventually earning a master's degree from Rutgers University-Newark.

When I first launched IRONBOUND Boxing, I was insecure about my lack of a formal business education. I didn't apply to business school because I didn't believe I was smart enough to get in. I took the SAT more than six times to get into the Naval Academy, and I was afraid of taking the GMAT, the graduate exam to get into business school. I always believed academics weren't my forte. At least, that's what I told myself. Now, I no longer say I honestly believe that, because I'm confident if I don't know the answer to something, I know how to find it and figure it out.

Being an entrepreneur has expanded my understanding of knowledge, education, and how to obtain both outside of the confines of a traditional classroom.

THE HUSTLER'S MBA

I start my morning each day with an audiobook or a podcast. I like to listen while I'm in the shower or brushing my teeth. For some reason, listening to audio while in the shower is my place of solace. Sometimes I find myself taking multiple showers a day, all for the experience of shutting off my mind and listening to some good educational content.

Who would've thought a shower could make an excellent classroom?

Once I'm dressed for the day, I grab a cup of coffee from the shop downstairs and make my way toward my office, located at an incubator space about ten to fifteen minutes from my apartment in the heart of downtown, Newark. It's just enough time to listen to a good dose of audio. During the mornings, I enjoy educational content the most, particularly the type that gives tactical advice such as how to develop a marketing strategy or build systems in your business.

Once I get to the office, I sit down and try to plan out my day before I start cranking away on the tasks that need to be done.

All throughout the day, I'm learning every chance I get, listening to podcasts on my way from lunch, during coffee breaks, and on my way to the IRONBOUND Boxing Academy in the evenings.

You don't have to be as aggressive with your learning as me, but you do need to adopt a habit of cultivating knowledge.

The pursuit of knowledge is your secret weapon to overcoming many of the challenges that are common amongst the Black entrepreneurial community, which we discussed previously.

HOW THIS APPLIES TO YOU:
- Start by researching books, podcasts, and videos on topics you're interested in to gain knowledge and information to apply to your venture.
- Connect with owners and employees in the industry your business is in. Be thoughtful and honest when reaching out.
- Take advantage of entrepreneurial education programs, including those specifically for veterans, founders of color, and other opportunities in your local community. Don't limit yourself to only veteran or minority programs, however.

ADDITIONAL RESOURCES:

READ
- *The Personal MBA: Master the Art of Business* by Josh Kauffman
- The Minimalist Entrepreneur: How Great Founders Do More with Less by Sahil Lavingia

LISTEN
- *Earn your Leisure* podcasts
- *The Transition* podcasts: "Always Be Learning"

16

DON'T GO AT IT ALONE, GET A BUSINESS COACH

*"Don't condemn if you see a person has a dirty glass of water,
[...] just show them the clean glass of water that you have.
When they inspect it, you won't have to say that yours is better."*

—ELIJAH MUHAMMAD

If a boxer told you they were going to compete for a national title without a coach, what would you say? I'm guessing it would be along the lines of, "That's really not a great idea." And boxing is a sport.

So when it comes to starting businesses, arguably one of the most important decisions of our lives, the last thing you may think about is seeking a business coach.

Nowadays I know better, having learned this lesson the hard way after years of going at it alone. Now the number one piece of advice I give entrepreneurs is to *get a business coach!*

I don't mean a charlatan you came across on YouTube who promises to help you make your first million in six months or less by producing some online courses. I mean a real business coach, one who's worked with hundreds, if not thousands, of entrepreneurs and who has developed a pattern recognition for how to launch and scale a successful business.

I remember my life before and after having a business coach, and it's night and day. Although I still describe entrepreneurship as making sausage, thanks to my coach Bill Watkins from The Lions Pride, at least I know what I'm doing while making the sausage.

MY FIRST BUSINESS COACH

I started seeking out a business coach in spring 2019. Although I have to admit at the time, I didn't know what a business coach was or that it was what I needed. I just knew I needed help.

Heading into the summer and coming off the high of a $25,000 grant I won from the Mark L. Rockefeller and the StreetShares Foundation, a nonprofit that inspires, educates, and supports the military entrepreneurial community, I burned out.

I allowed boxing to consume my life with no end in sight.

Every day I ran back and forth between New York City and Newark, splitting my time between coaching boxing for corporate clients and the kids at the IRONBOUND

Boxing Academy. I knew my lifestyle wasn't sustainable, especially given the fact I wasn't generating much revenue or donations.

Eventually, I reached out to Jack Fanous, the founder of the GI Go Fund, one of the largest nonprofit veteran organizations in the country and based in Newark, inquiring if he knew of an executive coach or someone I could work with.

For the last year, I was working out of the GI Go Fund's veteran incubator space, which they offered to veteran entrepreneurs and is currently home to my podcasts studio for IRONBOUND Media. Jack is a friend and mentor of mine, having created his own hybrid business model with a for-profit and nonprofit arm. I don't quite know why I initially asked for an executive coach, because I sure as hell didn't consider myself an executive at this point. Jack was one of my biggest supporters in Newark, and something told me he'd be a great resource to find a coach.

When I gave myself the title of founder and CEO, I was just going along with the crowd, like so many other entrepreneurs who give themselves such titles on social media and declare to the world, "Look at me, I'm an entrepreneur."

Me, an executive? Psshhh, I was a hustler, and I knew it.

Around the same time, I became close with Mike Nemeth, a West Point graduate and founder of Emblem Athletic. I'd talk with him on the phone as he conducted his cross-country road trips raising funds and delivering gear to clients. Mike mentioned he was heading to Jackson Hole, Wyoming, for some kind of get-together with a group of West Point graduates to work on his business. He didn't go into much detail at the time, but once I told him I was seeking a business coach, he recommended I get connected with his group, which I later found out was The Lions Pride.

Founded by Bill Watkins, an Army veteran, West Point graduate, and seasoned entrepreneur, The Lions Pride is a professional training coaching company for badass founders that serves mission-driven, high-performing, small business owners with at-the-ready resources, battle-tested tools, and full-service support.

Mike introduced me to Bill via email. He also included an entrepreneur named Trevor Shirk, another West Point graduate who I came across during my time consulting for WeWork.

Trevor and I are relatively the same age, both in the entrepreneur hustle, and both alumni of WeWork and Bunker Labs Veterans in Residence program.

Below is a follow up to Mike Nemeth's email introduction to Bill:

Hey Mike (N.), thanks for the introduction. I am honored by your trust and privileged to meet another badass you care about.

Hey Mike (S.), very energized to meet you. When Mike N. talks, I listen. I'm leaving for several weeks of unplugged PTO beginning tomorrow. How about you talk to Trevor Shirk (USMA '08), who's a cohort member (like Mike N.) and can help you understand what we do here and, more importantly, how you'd benefit.

I'm not sure what you might be looking for (if anything), or why Mike N. felt compelled to introduce us. I'll say this anyway: The Cohort and what we do here isn't for the faint of heart. Neither is a thriving business and an extraordinary life at the same time. Few get it, but inside here most do (or are headed that direction). I describe us like this: Grinding your way to success on your own or with a few buddies is a minivan. Might get you there depending on how fast you want to go. Reading books, listening to podcasts, attending conferences, and other development/coaching programs is a ZR1 Corvette. Well-engineered, fast, and right there at the top. What I'm proposing to you is Formula One. Not for everyone... actually, F! is for the very few elite. But this Ferrari is take-your-breath-away fast, effective... and totally worth it.

I've cc'd Trevor on this note just in case a quick call might be something you'd find valuable.

A few days later, I was heading to my incubator space when Trevor called. He barely got in a word before I blurted out, "Sign me up, I want in." At the time, Trevor was helping The Lions Pride with sales while buying out his cofounders from his own venture running a marketing agency that helped cannabis dispensaries dominate SEO. Business can burn you out, and he went through a hard time with his cofounders. While we spoke on the phone, Trevor opened up a little about his own business challenges and told me more about The Lions Pride, commonly referred to as the TLP.

Bill Watkins started the group after he sold his previous company, The Marena Group, a medical apparel company that created compression garments for burn victims and other skin ailments, which he sold for millions of dollars.

Originally, TLP was called the Rusty Lion Academy, catered to mid-level business executives seeking personal and career growth. Bill parted ways with his original cofounder and rebranded the business to TLP to focus on coaching service academy graduates like myself. Trevor arranged for Bill and me to talk that same day, and so I was able to jump on a quick fifteen minute call to let him know where I was at in my business.

I needed direction!

After our brief talk, Bill instructed me that Trevor would reach out again for the next steps. Not too long later, I received my invitation to a live-event in Jackson Hole, Wyoming, where they did quarterly planning and I'd have an opportunity to meet other members of the cohort. The only issue was it came with a hefty price tag.

At the time, TLP memberships were $1,000 a month, and I was paying myself approximately $3,500 a month from for-profit endeavors and not taking a salary from IRONBOUND Boxing. More than half my paycheck went toward rent and food, so needless to say, I wasn't exactly rolling in the dough. I learned either I'd have to pay the monthly membership fee or $3,000 to attend the event, which was otherwise free to active cohort members. I sat on that for a couple of days before deciding to pull the trigger, and as I look back on it today, it was without a doubt one of the best decisions of my life.

I knew I still had some funding left over from the Street-Shares grant and decided to allocate a significant portion of it to cover business coaching. I never imagined I could afford spending that much on coaching, but I had nothing to lose. I couldn't keep spinning on the entrepreneur hamster wheel. This was my first of many steps to get off it.

By September of that year, I found myself in Jackson Hole for the first time. I'm pretty sure I was the only Black person on the airplane. Funny enough, before I left, I mentioned to a couple of friends I was headed out to Jackson Hole, to which they responded, "Who the hell do you know out there?"

Jackson Hole was known as a place where rich white people went to avoid paying taxes, and only people in the know knew about Jackson Hole. This includes the Wall Street investments banking and private equity crowd with elite MBAs. Yet, here I was flying from Newark to Jackson Hole, which threw a few people off.

I spent the weekend at Bill's ranch, The Dragonfly Inn, a beautiful seven-bedroom house located on his private property with beautiful mountains in the background. In addition to me, there were several other veteran-owned small business owners, as well as locals running a variety of companies from construction, apparel, to CPG.

I'm not going to lie, I was slightly intimidated once I met the other members of The Lions Pride. By and large everyone was running a business generating at least $1 million-plus in revenue, and I had a nonprofit with approximately $10,000 in the bank account and what felt like a fledgling corporate wellness business. However, I learned a long time ago the importance of operating at the edge of your own competency, which I'd reached at that time. I also remembered the saying, "If you're surrounded by four broke friends, you're probably the fifth."

For the next three days, I learned the ins and outs of running a successful venture, including how to set your company's core purpose and core values, manage your team, and lead with intention. This wasn't just business advice, these were best practices that service academy founders, such as myself, had successfully implemented and reaped the rewards from. Although I felt slightly overwhelmed at first, I was all in.

We didn't spend the entire time focused only on business. We also focused on life and the importance of being intentional with our goals and aspirations, including our families. I had just entered a new relationship with my beautiful girlfriend, Symone Gates, and was struggling on how to balance it all. Thankfully, I wasn't the only one, and over the weekend we all opened up about our different struggles and how to overcome them. We talked around the dinner table, at the fire pit, and on hikes.

It was a great opportunity to let my guard down and pull back the curtain on my life.

By the end of the weekend I felt confident, connected, and empowered to return to Newark and continue what I had set out to do with IRONBOUND Boxing. Upon my return, it initially felt like I was staring at a pile of rubble and had to turn it into a pyramid, and even though I didn't feel like I knew exactly what I was doing, I did have a plan.

The first thing I did was sit down at my computer and build out IRONBOUND Boxing's brand playbook, creating our core values, core purpose, bold beliefs, and everything else. Each of these included principles and philosophies to get to the essence of why IRONBOUND Boxing exists. Next, I sent out invites to a select group of people and organized my board of directors, something I had planned to do for years but never got around to. I built an operating system for the nonprofit, using the tools I received from TLP, and gave my team marching orders.

I had a tribe, tools, and the support I needed to excel now.

Despite the challenges the next few years would bring, the TLP served as my secret weapon, helping me navigate the chaos of the pandemic and stay in the fight. Although the next few years were challenging, I drastically improved my confidence and business acumen, leading IRONBOUND Boxing and raising over $100,000 for the first time ever in the midst of a global pandemic while simultaneously launching IRONBOUND Media, thanks to Bill and The Lions Pride.

Since joining the TLP in September 2019, I've traveled to Jackson Hole at least eight or more times. I've lost count at this point because I fly out every quarter for quarterly planning. In addition, I attend weekly coaching calls with my cohort and talk with Bill multiple times a week. We're constantly emailing and shooting text messages back and forth, where we go over different business strategies or merely share general advice. I even have the privilege of cohosting the *Dog Whistle Branding* podcasts with him.

After having a business coach in my corner, I won't start another venture without one. Entrepreneurship is too hard to go at it alone. Mentorship is great, but having a coach who is committed to seeing you succeed and doing everything in their power to see you do so is invaluable.

THE BOOK PUBLISHING LADY

Renee Bobb is a serial entrepreneur based in Nashville, Tennessee, where she runs multiple ventures, including an independent publishing company, a training and development consultancy, and a semi-pro women's basketball team. As a former telecommunications operator in the Navy, Renee transitioned off active duty to pursue her passion for entrepreneurship.

One of the keys to Renee's success has been her willingness to constantly seek knowledge and tutelage under a professional business coach.

As an athlete in the Navy playing for the North Atlantic Treaty Organization basketball team, Renee is accustomed to having coaches on and off the court.

She's always had someone in her ear, correcting her form and helping her reach her potential so she can get to the next level. In addition, access to her coaches gives her tools, updates her with new information, and helps her scale.

Renee has multiple business coaches, one to challenge her, one to let her vent and whine, and another to nourish her spirit. She has such big dreams and aspirations that she needs her coaches to keep her accountable on the different aspects of her life and businesses she aims to improve.

Because I'm an athlete, I've always had a coach, right? You know, from middle school to playing in the Staten Island Basketball Association. Since I was younger, I've always had someone in my ear, always amplifying the good things that I have within myself. So it just kind of made sense that as I began to make the transition to entrepreneurship to have someone who could do the same thing. Someone who's able to give me some new tools and information I can use to scale what it is I'm doing.

Outside of professional coaches, which come at a cost, she also takes advantage of advisors at the Nashville Entrepreneur Center. As a member, she receives access to over three hundred advisors who give one hour of their time at no cost. This allows her to go to specific advisors for specific things, such as financial and acquisition experts.

Working with business coaches and advisors allows Renee to avoid the mistakes others have made and accelerates her learning and her success.

Renee credits coaching with her entrepreneurial success and allowing her to pay it forward to hosting small business development for underrepresented minorities. She currently serves as the head of training and development at Bunker Labs where she oversees *The Breaking Barriers in Entrepreneurship* workshop series. Outside of Bunker Labs, she runs similar programs for government agencies and corporations committed to supporting small businesses.

HOW THIS APPLIES TO YOU:

- Start seeking out a business coach. You can expect to pay anywhere between five hundred to fifteen hundred a month for a good coach. I know this sounds daunting, but if you find the right one, you'll increase your investment ten times.
- Probe your network. Ask successful entrepreneurs within your friend group or personal network if they have a coach and whether or not they recommend if he or she would be a good fit for you.
- Look at their track record of success. Find out what other entrepreneurs they've worked with and their success rate. Ideally, your coach should have industry experience in your targeted space or is tied heavily into a community you're a part of, in my case, service academy graduates and veterans.
- They should be accessible. Your coach and their team should make time for you. A good coach isn't someone you pay a one-time fee and never see or hear from them again. Online modules and courses are great at times, but you need to be able to leverage one-on-one or, at the very least, group interaction.

- They should have a coach of their own. A good coach is always learning. If your coach is a know-it-all and doesn't have a group or coach advising them, that's a giant red flag. Some of the best coaches I know are part of elite mastermind groups that empower them and make sure they are delivering the best value to those they serve.

ADDITIONAL RESOURCES:

READ

- *Passion Purpose Profit: Sidestep the Hustle and Build A Business You Love* by Fionna Killackey. (This is the closest thing to having a business coach in a book!)
- *The No. B.S. Small Business Book: How to Win When Most Fail* by Casey Graham

LISTEN

- *The Transition* podcasts: "How To 10X Your Business with Army Veteran Bill Watkins, Founder of The Lions Pride"
- *The Transition* podcasts: "Breaking Barriers in Entrepreneurship with Navy Veteran and Serial Entrepreneur Renee Bob, National Director of Training and Development at Bunker Labs"

17

FIND ADVISORS

"All business is personal, make friends before you need them."

—ROBERT L. JOHNSON

I once heard a quote, "If you want to go to the Super Bowl, recruit a team of players who've been there before." The same concept applies in business, except replace the "A" in team with advisors.

When you first launch your venture, it can be difficult to recruit talent, especially when you can't afford to hire them. However, you can surround yourself with a network of advisors who understand the industry you're targeting and can provide support, such as access to vendors, potential clients, and resources to help you grow. Unlike your business coach, your advisors should be business owners or subject matter experts.

Business advisors allow you to cover gaps in your business, such as sales and marketing, and provide strategic guidance to keep you and your team in the fight.

Between the internet and social media platforms like LinkedIn and Twitter, it's never been easier to find and connect with potential advisors in your industry.

You just have to know what you need and where to look.

THE ACADEMY INVESTOR NETWORK

My fraternity brother and Navy veteran, Sherman Williams, always wanted to be in venture capital. Sherman, like many veterans, felt he needed more formal training before entering that world. Therefore, he spent several years in investment banking before starting his own venture capital firm.

From the very beginning, he knew he did not want to do it alone. A former investment banker with an MBA from the Booth School of Business at The University of Chicago, Sherman's passion for venture stems from his passion to make an impact by investing in founders trying to make the world a better place.

I have always been a "people person," and I truly get inspired by people who are trying to change the world for the better.

While working full-time in mergers and acquisitions in healthcare banking, Sherman advised and invested in start-ups on the side to get his feet wet. Between his investment activities and the relationships he built on Wall Street, Sherman established a strong reputation and network of mentors to support him once he decided to take the big leap, none more important than fellow veteran Bradley Harrison.

Bradley is an Army veteran, West Point graduate, and the founder and managing partner of Scout Ventures, an early-stage venture capital firm making the world a better, safer place by investing in frontier and dual-use technologies built by veterans, intelligence leaders, and premier research labs.

Sherman met Bradley through a fellow Naval Academy classmate, Wesley Blackwell. As Sherman began to explore the idea of starting his own venture fund, Bradley and Wesley approached him about leading an angel syndicate, a group of investors that invest together, specifically comprised of Academy grads and veterans.

Sherman took the idea and ran with it.

Bradley and Wesley also introduced and suggested he partner up with Emily McMahan, also an Army veteran and West Point graduate with a track record of working and advising early-stage founders.

Although a venture doesn't have the same structure or business model as a small business or startup, it's a venture nonetheless, and this was Sherman's first one.

Together, under the tutelage of Bradley, Sherman and Emily, they officially launched The Academy Investor Network, first as an angel syndicate organizing veterans from all across the country to invest in other veteran founders. Approximately one year after starting the syndicate, they established AIN Ventures, an early-stage venture fund that invests in dual-use technology and veteran-led start-ups.

In addition to the guidance and mentorship from Bradley, Scout Ventures became the first investor in the AIN Fund.

During a podcast interview on their show, *Those Who Dare*, Sherman stated, "Bradley has a great deal of experience relative to Emily and I, and the data he has gathered via these experiences enables him to provide us with a tremendous amount of guidance."

Since officially launching in 2020, AIN has gone on to receive a $2.5 million investment from USAA, along with additional investments from limited partners across the country.

With Bradley's and his cofounder Emily's support, AIN is on the move. Sherman feels prepared for success and is fulfilled in every way.

THE DIFFERENCE BETWEEN ADVISORS AND MENTORS

I view advisors as having a more formal stake in the outcome of your business, as opposed to mentors.

In the example above, Bradley is a seasoned venture capitalist who knows firsthand the challenges it takes to raise a fund and what to look for in founders. Not only did he provide mentorship to Emily and Sherman, he also invested in them financially.

Don't get me wrong, mentors are great, but the relationship is often a lot less informal. You can call mentors on the phone, grab dinner, and have any other casual interactions. Advisors, on the other hand, will get in the weeds with you and conduct whiteboard sessions.

MY EXPERIENCE WITH ADVISORS

Over the years, I've worked with several advisors for both IRONBOUND Boxing and IRONBOUND Media.

After I returned from Stanford Ignite in the summer of 2017, I took a class on social entrepreneurship at Rutgers Business School, taught by Dr. Jeffrey Robinson. Up until that point, I felt like I was living in a bubble trying to sell people on my vision to change the world through boxing.

I spent the next four months learning the various different business models for social enterprises, including nonprofits, benefit corporations, and traditional businesses. Dr. Robinson's passion for teaching and the exposure I received on the social impact movement gave me the courage to leave my full-time job and focus on the next phase of IRONBOUND Boxing.

When I did, I immediately reached out to Dr. Robinson to be my official advisor. For the next several months, I met with him in the lobby of Rutgers Business School, discussing our business model and how I should approach building the brand. To assist me, he made introductions on my behalf, along with the opportunity for several speaking engagements, including the opportunity to be featured on a panel at the New Jersey Social Impact Summit.

The benefit of having Dr. Robinson in my corner is his knowledge of the social impact movement, including support and funding opportunities. He's one of the most highly respected educational professionals in the space, and my ability to consistently call him on the phone and pick his brain is invaluable.

The same goes for my advisor with IRONBOUND Media, Christopher Lochhead, who I mentioned in the chapter on positioning. I met Chris through Twitter after reading his book, *Play Bigger*. I sent him a tweet asking to discuss how to implement his teachings amongst veteran and under-represented founders, particularly around category design and brand building.

As a three-time chief marketing officer with a number one podcast and book, Chris knows more than a thing or two about what it takes to build a successful brand.

Chris immediately responded to my tweet and sent me a direct message containing his phone number. He instructed me to give him a call.

For the next two hours, we spoke on the phone about all things IRONBOUND and my new plans for IRONBOUND Media. He made himself available to talk via phone and text whenever I needed him, and for the next two years he taught me everything he knows about category design, podcasting, and how to build a successful business. He even gave me a pep talk on how to sell!

Another advisor who comes to mind is Peter Kestenbaum, a retired business executive and angel investor, who has also been in my corner since 2018. We met through a local entrepreneur program at the New Jersey Institute of Technology. Peter has a strong background in marketing and business development. He literally had to walk me through how to set up my first sales dashboard for IRONBOUND Boxing. He also gave me the nudge and confidence to write this book.

Advisors are an invaluable asset for BVE's. Don't overlook them.

COVER YOUR GAPS

When it comes to seeking out advisors, start by covering your gaps and looking for areas you lack expertise.

Up until I started IRONBOUND Boxing, I didn't know the first thing about standing up a nonprofit organization. The Academy was one thing, but the organizational structure was an entirely different beast. Rather than remaining ignorant, I leaned on Dr. Robinson and others.

It's not rocket science.

In the Marine Corps we have a saying: "Know yourself and seek self-improvement." So if you don't know something, find someone who does.

Find your advisors!

HOW THIS APPLIES TO YOU:

- Look for individuals within your network or third-party connections with experience in sales, marketing, and all other related fields.
- Try to find advisors with specific industry expertise in the niche you're targeting, i.e., woman-owned CPG companies.
- Set a consistent check-in cadence for accountability purposes.
- Keep your initial group of advisors small in order to create more intimate relationships.

ADDITIONAL RESOURCES:

READ

- *Harvard Business Review*: "Who Advises the Entrepreneur?" by Kerrie MacPherson
- *Built to Scale: How Top Companies Create Breakthrough Growth Through Exceptional Advisory Boards* by Marissa Levin

LISTEN

- *The Transition* podcasts: "How to Organize an Advisory Board"

18

FIND YOUR PEOPLE

"If you want to go fast go alone, if you want to go far, go together."

—AFRICAN PROVERB

Starting a business is hard enough as it is without trying to go at it alone. That's one of the reasons why so many founders love the idea of starting a business with a cofounder or team, so when times get rough, they have someone to lean on.

As military veterans, we come from a culture of operating in units and teams. At any given time, we always had a swim or battle buddy watching our backs and holding us accountable. As entrepreneurs, it's our responsibility to seek out our own community and accountability partners.

And if they don't exist, we have to build them from the ground up.

MECH VENTURES

After years of working in the venture capital space, Air Force veteran Mario Mitchell and military brat Bruce Hamiton decided to launch their own firm Mech Ventures, an early-stage venture capital firm that invests in the future of pop culture.

Mech Ventures is based in Las Vegas, which presents its own set of challenges for an emerging Black-led VC firm.

We're the only Black VC firm in Nevada, which means I don't have many people I can fall back on to talk about the struggles that we're going through.

Without a local Black VC network to lean on, Mario turned to the internet and found his community on Twitter, connecting and engaging with other Black venture capitalists who share the struggles of running their firms.

I'm on Twitter a lot more now because of the VC space... I've been a big fan of Mac Conwell, from Rare Breed Ventures. I love everything he puts out there. Not only does he look like me, but he shares the struggle of learning and growing and having a cool community around to help him grow.

Outside of Twitter and before Mech Ventures, Mario began cultivating a tribe of veteran entrepreneurs. After hearing about Bunker Labs, Mario knew he needed a tribe in Las Vegas, and he took the initiative to stand up Bunker Labs Las Vegas.

Through his efforts cultivating the veteran entrepreneur community, he gained the attention of local investors, so when it came time to start Mech Ventures he had a support network to build upon.

Today, Mech Venture is a rolling fund with approximately $10 million under management and growing. "We're sharing all our knowledge, and all the people who are helping us build Mech… that's how you grow a truly dope ecosystem."

I can't stress enough the importance of finding and joining a community.

As far as I'm concerned, it's non-negotiable for BVEs. Communities make you feel like you're part of a tribe, where everyone looks out for one another and there's a commitment to surviving and thriving together.

A strong community feels like a family, where you can be vulnerable while also building a network you're able to activate and rally support around your business.

The elements of a strong community include:
- A group of individuals who share the same interests and values as you
- Frequent online or in-person meetings to maintain connection with one another
- A genuine interest in being supportive and helpful to one another

Entrepreneurship is lonely.

The only thing I've found as equally lonely is serving as a platoon commander in the Marines. For any of us who have been in any sort of leadership position, we have to make decisions that affect others on a constant basis. Unfortunately, not all the decisions we make are good ones, and we have the burden of responsibility that comes with the mistakes.

In the military, we carried the ultimate responsibility of caring for others' lives and well-being. The same applies to our businesses. Even if you don't have any employees, you still have clients, customers, and your family who are relying on you.

This brings immense pressure, and you need communities that understand this burden and can help you navigate it.

ONLINE COMMUNITIES

The internet has opened up a world of possibilities when it comes to community building. Between social media, online forums like Reddit, and YouTube, it's never been easier to find an online community.

You just have to know where to look and be willing to go the extra mile by joining and engaging with community members. A great option is online communities and private groups found on platforms including Slack, Discord, and more recently, Circles.

I'm a part of multiple private Slack channels that allow me to engage with veteran entrepreneurs and non-ventured-back tech start-ups, or what are commonly called indie entrepreneurs. For years, I've communicated back and forth online with entrepreneurs who I've met in person, and we still manage to support one another.

In November, I joined an online community called Mega-Maker, a community of bootstrapped founders started in 2013. MegaMaker is for bootstrapped tech entrepreneurs, the majority who are building online products and software. The founder of MegaMaker is Justin Jackson, an indie entrepreneur who has launched multiple start-ups and podcasts. After following Justin's personal blog, podcasts, and various other content, I came across Mega-Maker and decided to join. I post and engage members a couple times a week, whether it's sharing wins or asking questions about marketing, design, or anything else.

While MegaMaker is a fully online community, The Lions Pride and Bunker Labs offer a hybrid-approach.

Not only do both organizations offer in-person programming, they also offer online training sessions and community channels to engage with other members throughout the week.

When I'm not flying to Jackson Hole for quarterly planning with The Lions Pride, I'm engaging with the members on Slack or Zoom.

Friday for the last two years, I've met with my acceleration partner from The Lions Pride, Ron Mouw, a fellow entrepreneur and West Point graduate. We started meeting during the pandemic to talk about life, business, and everything in between and haven't looked back since. And even after meeting for two years straight, we still haven't met in person. Still, Ron is one of the most trustworthy individuals I've ever met. Whenever I have a business problem I need to think through, I look forward to our calls to discuss it with him.

I remember talking with him in May of 2020 about my aspirations to launch a podcast company even before I knew what it would look like. Ron helped me think through the initial business plan, and the next thing he knew I was off to the races.

The key is having someone you can go to.

IN-PERSON MEET-UPS

In-person meet-ups are a great way to get plugged into an ecosystem and start building your network. While it's great to maintain communication with your network online and over social media platforms, there's nothing better than meeting people in person.

For the longest time I had reservations about attending conferences, given the travel cost and time commitment. But once I realized my perfect customer was military veterans, I decided to attend the Military Veteran Start-up Conference in San Francisco, hosted by Context Ventures.

For forty-eight hours, military veterans ascended on the Marines' Memorial Club Hotel in San Francisco to fellowship and network with one another. The conference included panels on venture capital, consumer companies, and nonprofits.

Participants flew in from all over the country, from New York to Utah, in order to attend the inaugural conference. I enjoyed the opportunity to connect with veteran entrepreneurs I admire, like Randy Hetrix, founder of TRX, the performance workout equipment bands.

Conferences aren't the only opportunity to connect in-person. You can take advantage of meet-up opportunities in your local community.

For example, if you love cooking and have aspirations of opening your own restaurant one day, look for opportunities in your local community where food entrepreneurs meet. You can find them with a simple google search.

Be sure to also follow social media accounts and influencers in your area of industry. Oftentimes they promote events taking place, either online or in-person.

Conferences are also another great way to get out and start meeting people. There's entrepreneurial conferences for military veterans, indie founders, women entrepreneurs... you name it. Although many of these conferences come with a price tag, between travel and event costs, they're a great way to connect with people offline.

For the longest time, like I said, I was skeptical of conferences, until I realized they are a great way to bring people together at one time in the same location. In these times, it can be hard to get multiple people in the same place at any given time, especially when we're spread out all over the country.

Attending a conference takes care of that.

DON'T BE AFRAID OF NETWORKING

Networking often gets a bad rap because for a lot of entrepreneurs, it can be purely transactional, i.e., I'm only networking with you because I want to do business someday, as opposed to genuinely enjoying someone else's company whether you do business together or not. When we go out of our way to network and don't feel like it's translating to revenue, it can feel like a waste of time.

That's why I encourage you to be more intentional about who you choose to network with and what you hope to accomplish.

Look for networking opportunities that go beyond the superficial and allow you to spend time with people who not only share similar interests as you but similar values.

If physical fitness and mental health are important to you, look for groups that encourage both.

At The Lions Pride, we embrace a culture of health and wellness. It's not just about business. We believe healthy bodies lead to a healthy mind. At every live-event I attend, there are healthy snacks available, some form of wellness activity, and healthy meals cooked by an in-person chef.

While attending TLP events, I know I don't have to compromise my health. We prioritize health.

If family is important to you, look for groups that provide a family friendly environment, such as picnics, barbecues, and other fun activities. It's important to set boundaries for yourself so you have a better understanding of what to look for in a community. If weekends are off limits due to family obligations, find a community that meets online or during the week.

MAXIMIZE YOUR PARTICIPATION IN COMMUNITIES BY LEARNING ABOUT OTHER MEMBERS AND HOW TO HELP THEM WIN

In every community you join, your goal should be to add value. Everyone brings different experiences and expertise, which other community members can benefit from. Look for opportunities to add value in their lives by sharing knowledge, resources, and other helpful information.

Don't be selfish and only take from the community, always asking other members "What can you do for me?" Instead, figure out what you can do for them.

If you want to win, start by helping others win first. The best way I've found to network is to connect people with one another. A simple introduction over email or LinkedIn goes a long way.

Whenever I come across a new connection at an event or online, I make a habit of asking them about their business and what challenges they are currently facing. That way, as I come across opportunities in my network, I can forward them their way.

I recently came across a veteran entrepreneur who was relaunching his creative agency, working with brands to help increase their online presence through website, SEO, and other digital forms. When a mentor of mine reached out asking if I knew anyone who did websites, I immediately connected the two. It took me less than two minutes to draft the email and help the veteran get a new client.

To get the most out of networking, you have to understand it's about people helping people.

If you know someone is looking for a graphic designer to help with their logo and you know of a graphic designer in your local community or one you've worked with previously, simply connect them. It might not seem like much now, but the people you help will remember.

I've lost count of the number of times I've helped someone and it's come back to me in a positive way, whether an introduction to a potential prospect, funding opportunity, or just genuine goodwill.

In 2019, I won a $25,000 grant from the StreetShares Foundation. In order to win the grant, I had to obtain online votes, which I raised via social media. I placed in the top three and pitched in-person in Washington, DC, which required more voting to win first place. I credit the win with the amount of goodwill I built over the years helping other veteran entrepreneurs. When I asked them to vote for me or share my posts on social media, many of them went above and beyond.

Too often, we only go to people when we need something instead of cultivating relationships over time.

Sometimes you have to start planting the seeds now that you can benefit from later. Don't wait.

Start aligning yourself with individuals and organizations with shared interests and values today. As BVEs, when times get rough over the course of your entrepreneurial journey, your community will be the place you go to vent, keep you sane, and learn from others in similar positions as you.

HOW THIS APPLIES TO YOU:
- Understand you can't go at it alone, so look for opportunities to connect with other entrepreneurs either online or in-person.
- Make a habit of making introductions on behalf of other founders, with the expectation to receive nothing in return.
- When you find yourself in a rut and things aren't going your way, go to your community and be vulnerable. Don't be afraid to ask for help.

ADDITIONAL RESOURCES:

READ
- *Get Together: How to Build a Community with Your People* by Bailey Richardson, Kevin Huynh, Kai Elmer Sotto

- *Tribe: On Homecoming and Belonging* by Sebastian Junger

LISTEN
- *The Transition* podcasts: "The Importance of Community"

19

BUILD YOUR SUPPORT NETWORK

"Never eat with the people you didn't starve with. Never ride with the people you didn't walk with. Be true and stick to your crew."

—UNKNOWN

When you're going to war, you need a squad you can rely on and trust to have your back, especially when times get rough. The same applies in business and the support network you build around yourself.

I view a support network different from general networking, because what I'm encouraging you to do is build an A-team of reliable companies, contractors, and vendors you can call on in a moment's notice. When you need to purchase products and services for your company or make referrals on behalf of others, your support network are the people whom you can trust and do business with.

THE DESIGN COMPANY

There's no way I'd be in the position I am today if it wasn't for the amazing support network around me. When I was first starting out, I barely had any money and didn't know what I was doing, despite a lot of the early success IRON-BOUND Boxing received in the press. Thankfully, multiple entrepreneurs stepped up to the plate to show their support, helping me launch our first website, create apparel, and so much more. Now, as a return of favor, every chance I get I hire them for work or make referrals on their behalf.

In April of 2017, I met Drew O'Brien at a Bunker Labs event in New York City. Drew is a graphic designer and the founder of The Design Company, a full-service marketing agency that builds brands that get customer's attention at first sight.

Although not a veteran, Drew consistently allocates time to work with and help veteran-owned businesses pro bono. Once he heard about the work I was doing with IRONBOUND Boxing through mutual friends, he came to the Bunker Labs event to formally introduce himself.

Drew approached me and said, "Hey man, I love everything you are doing with IRONBOUND Boxing. I've been following you from afar and want you to know if there's anything I can do to help, let me know."

"Thanks, man. I really appreciate it," I responded.

Drew handed me his business card. A few weeks later, I contacted him and grabbed lunch at Montclair Diner, an upscale diner in Montclair, New Jersey, just up the street from Drew's office at the time.

Drew pulled out a black notebook full of sketches and designs he was working on. I could tell he was serious about his craft.

He said, "So here's the deal, man: I believe in what you're doing, and I want to make time to help you. Tell me everything about IRONBOUND Boxing—your goals, vision, everything."

For the next hour and half, I shared my ambition for building a nationally recognized brand in the heart of Newark. I told him about my background as an amateur boxer, why I fell in love with the sport, and why I believed kids should train for free. I shared with Drew my vision for creating a logo that's nationally recognized and worn on gear and apparel in communities across the country. I showed him different sports brands including Everlast and their sister company, Lonsdale, and I let him work his magic.

Drew took notes, and at the end of lunch he told me he'd get back to me and see what he can do.

A few weeks later, Drew sent me an email with new logos and brand guidelines for IRONBOUND Boxing. Instantly I was blown away. "Dude, this is the sickest thing I've ever seen!"

He rebranded our original design into something more classic that could stand next to Everlast, Nike, and other iconic sports brands. Drew did all of this out of the kindness of his heart, and from that moment on, I knew he was my guy.

Almost five years after our initial lunch meeting, Drew is still my number one design guy. Drew created the podcasts cover art for Dog Whistle Branding, helped me with the IRONBOUND Boxing website, and always provides a second set of eyes on all things branding.

I text Drew weekly and send him referrals every chance I get. It's been my goal to grow and have people I can rely on in my corner.

RELATIONSHIPS ARE EVERYTHING

The strength of your business is based on the strength of your relationships. Maintaining relationships requires work and cultivation. When I look around my support network and see guys like Drew, I'm thankful I took time to cultivate and maintain them over the years. In my mind, I refer to my network as the IRONBOUND collective. At any given time, I keep lists of graphic designers, lawyers, and entrepreneurs I'm constantly championing.

Strong support networks are like having a super power. At any given time you can go out to someone within your network to help you solve a problem, in your own business or someone else's.

HOW THIS APPLIES TO YOU:

- Build a collection of trustworthy business owners and vendors you can rely on.
- Establish frequent communication with one another in order to keep each other up to date on what's going on in your businesses.
- Share thoughts and ideas on your approach to your business so your A-team understands how you think and can evangelize your business in your absence.

ADDITIONAL RESOURCES:

READ

- *Who Not How: The Formula to Achieve Bigger Goals through Accelerating Teamwork* by Dan Sullivan and Dr. Benjamin Hardy
- *The Go-Giver, Expanded Edition: A Little Story About a Powerful Business Idea* by Bob Burg and John David Mann

LISTEN

- *The Transition* podcast: "How to Increase Your Revenue by Being a Go-Giver with Bob Burg, Author of *The Go-Giver*"
- *The Transition* podcast: "Why Relationships and Respect Are the Ultimate Currency in Business with Thomas Schwab, Chief Evangelist Officer of Interview Valet"

CONCLUSION

THE RISE OF
BLACK VETERAN
ENTREPRENEURS

"The Talented Tenth rises and pulls all that are worth the saving up to their vantage ground. This is the history of human progress; and the two historic mistakes which have hindered that progress were the thinking first that no more could ever rise save the few already risen; or second, that it would better the uprisen to pull the risen down."

—W.E.B. DU BOIS

As a Black veteran entrepreneur, you're the closest thing we have to the talented tenth, the belief an exceptional group of Black Americans will uplift the race.

When prominent Black scholar, author, and social critic W.E.B. Du Bois introduced the concept of the talented tenth in the early twentieth century, he was looking toward other Black scholars, civil rights leaders, and Black entrepreneurs.

Back then, Black veterans didn't have the knowledge and resources available today.

If Du Bois was still alive and saw the potential of our community, I like to think he, too, would look toward BVEs.

The time is ours, and it's on us to capitalize upon it. We can't wait on anyone else.

Our community faces serious challenges, including a growing wealth gap, apathetic youth, and poverty all around us.

As someone who lives in the heart of an inner-city, I'm worried about Black Americans' ability to compete for twenty-first century jobs, especially those requiring tech backgrounds. With rising inflation and increased cost of living, so many of our people are being left behind.

That's what fuels me to build the IRONBOUND Courage Academy, a place where kids can come train for free but also have access to an amazing coworking space and programming, including entrepreneurship and work-force development.

Deep down, Americans are begging for a talented tenth to attack the issues facing our community head on. My hope is that through your ventures, you can create wealth and impact that addresses many of them.

In his book, *Purple Cow: Transform Your Business by Being Remarkable*, Seth Godin states, "Ideas that spread are more likely to succeed than those that don't. I call ideas that spread idea viruses."

The belief that BVEs are our nation's biggest untapped resource is an idea worth spreading. But I can't do it alone. I need your help by implementing the ideas discussed in this book, getting results, and sharing what you learned with other BVEs far and wide.

On your way to the top, you must lift as you climb, whether it's helping other BVEs or Black Americans in your local community. If you don't, who else will?

Whether we still wear a uniform or not, we still have an opportunity to serve our country as BVEs.

I barely scratched the surface with this book. I know there are more BVEs out there, fighting the good fight without the spotlight.

We are a fraternity and sorority within a larger fraternity and sorority with limitless potential, and my hope is this book shines a light on it.

While you have come to the end of this book, you have come to the beginning of the conversation and the beginning of the BVE community.

Both the conversation and community continue at BlackVeteranEntrepreneurs.com and in our newsletter, BlackVeteranEntrepreneurs.Substack.com.

Visit the website to learn more about BVEs and subscribe to the newsletter to stay up to date with the latest BVE happenings, information, tools, and resources.

BVEs, it's time to rise up and step into our greatness.

Our people need us.

ACKNOWLEDGMENTS

Over the years I have had countless people pour into me, from my family and friends to strangers through random acts of kindness. Unfortunately, there is no book big enough to fit all the names.

As I reflect on this book writing journey, I cannot help but feel thankful.

I'm thankful for you taking the time to read my thoughts and participate in this author journey with me. I'm thankful for the countless mentors over the years, many I never met in person but consistently give me inspiration through podcasts, books, and blog articles. I'm thankful for those of you who supported the pre-sale campaign, making this book possible.

I'm thankful for my mother, Willeen Steadman, and my aunt, Betty Mitchell, for teaching me how to "lift as I climb."

I'm thankful for my friend and coauthor, Alana M. Abernethy, for being in my corner and helping me at every step along the way.

I'm thankful and humbled by the amazing veteran entrepreneur community that's carried me on its shoulders over the years, supporting all my endeavors from Fighting Mojo to IRONBOUND Boxing.

Lastly, I'm thankful for the opportunity to cultivate the next generation of BVEs.

ABOUT THE AUTHORS

"IRON" Mike Steadman

Mike is a serial entrepreneur based in Newark, New Jersey, committed to improving the economic and social outcomes of urban youth and military veterans through boxing, entrepreneurship, and news media.

He's the founder and CEO of IRONBOUND Boxing, a nonprofit that provides free amateur boxing training, entrepreneur education, and employment opportunities for Newark youth and young adults. Mike and his partner, Keith Colon, oversee the legendary IRONBOUND Boxing Academy, their free boxing gym for youth in Newark. He also runs IRONBOUND Media, a podcast production company that produces branded podcasts for veteran-owned businesses.

Mike is a three-time National Collegiate Boxing Champion from the United States Naval Academy and Marine Corps infantry officer, with deployments to Afghanistan and Japan/Philippines. He's currently a Hoover Institution Veteran Fellow at Stanford University, a public policy think tank promoting the principles of individual, economic, and political freedom.

His goal is to raise $1.5 million to build the first-ever IRONBOUND Courage Academy, a 5,000-square-foot boxing facility and small business incubator space for Newark's youth and young adults.

Through his efforts growing IRONBOUND Boxing and IRONBOUND Media, Mike has established himself as a high-profile veteran advocate and the new face of social entrepreneurship.

To learn more, visit www.IRONBOUNDBoxing.org and www.IRONBOUNDMedia.com

Alana M. Abernethy

Alana is an entrepreneur and writer. She's had a passion for and has understood the power of reading and writing from a young age.

While at the Naval Academy, she continued her passion for the writing arts, earning her Bachelor of Science in English, and graduated in the great Class of 2010 with a commission in the United States Navy as a Surface Warfare officer.

She will continue her studies and passion for writing in Columbia University's School of Journalism in the Class of 2024.

During her time in the Navy, Alana started her own publishing company and published her poetry collections.

Alana considers herself ultra-creative and committed to showing others the power of sharing their stories.

She plans to help more BVEs do just that.

APPENDIX

INTRODUCTION

- House Small Business Committee. "Committee Report Outlines COVID's Devastating Impact on Black-Owned Small Businesses." House Small Businesses Committee, press release, February 26, 2021. https://smallbusiness.house.gov/news/documentquery.aspx.

- Maury, Rosalinda, Mirza Tihic, Najla Almissalati. "2021 Data Brief: Black and African-American Veteran Entrepreneurs." New York: Institute for Veterans and Military Families at Syracuse University, 2021.

CHAPTER 2: THE ROAD AHEAD

- Churchill, Neil and Virginia, Lewis. "The Five Stages of Small Business Growth." *Harvard Business Review*, May, 1983.

CHAPTER 4: THE SIMPLIFIED BUSINESS PLAN

- Clear, James. *Atomic Habits: An Easy & Proven Way to Build Good Habits & Break Bad Ones*. New York: Avery, 2018.

- U.S. Census Bureau. *American Community Survey 5-year estimates.* Retrieved from Census Reporter Profile page for Newark, NJ. 2020. http://censusreporter.org/profiles/16000US3451000-newark-nj/.

CHAPTER 5: FIND YOUR PERFECT CUSTOMER

- Carter, Timothy. "The True Failure Rate of Small Businesses: Understanding how and why businesses fail can help prepare you for success." *Entrepreneur,* January 21, 2021.

- Weiss, Alan. *Getting Started in Consulting, 4th Ed.* New York: Wiley, April 2, 2019.

CHAPTER 6: BUILD YOUR BRAND

- Sinek, Simon. *Start With Why: How Great Leaders Inspire Everyone to Take Action.* Harlow, England: Penguin, 2009.

CHAPTER 7: POSITION YOURSELF OR BE POSITIONED

- Cole, Nicolas, Christopher Lochead, and Eddie Yoon. "DAM The Demand: How To Redesign Your Category And Take 76% Of The Market." *Category Pirates* (blog). January 1, 2022. https://categorypirates.substack.com/p/how-to-dam-the-demand-redesign-your.

- Dunford, April. "Don't Let Customers Decide What Your Product Is." *April Dunford* (blog). July 1, 2022. https://www.aprildunford.com/post/dont-let-customers-decide-what-your-product-is.

- Jackson, Justin. "Business is Like Surfing." *Justin Jackson* (blog). July 1, 2022. https://justinjackson.ca/surfing.

- Ramadan, Alan, Christopher Lochhead, Dave Peterson, and Kevin Maney. *Play Bigger: How Pirates, Dreamers, and Innovators Create and Dominate Markets.* New York: Harper, 2016.

- Walling, Rob. *Start Small, Stay Small: A Developers Guide To Launching A Startup.* California: Numa Group, 2010.

- Yoon, Eddie, and Linda Deeken. "Why It Pays to Be a Category Creator." *Harvard Business Review.* March 2013.

CHAPTER 9: THE CUSTOMER ACTIVATION CYCLE

- *Designing the Future of Education* (blog). "Steph Manuel (MMM '19) Shares How MMM Prepared Him to Launch TrueFiktion in an Effort to Redesign How People Understand and Relate to American History." February 17, 2022. https://design.northwestern.edu/mmm-program/inside-our-program/stories/2022/designing-the-future-of-history-education.html.

CHAPTER 10: HOW TO ACQUIRE YOUR FIRST TEN CUSTOMERS & BEYOND

- Cole, Nicolas, Christopher Lochead, and Eddie Yoon. "DAM The Demand: How To Redesign Your Category And Take 76% Of The Market." *Category Pirates* (blog), January 1, 2022. https://categorypirates.substack.com/p/how-to-dam-the-demand-redesign-your.

- Godin, Seth. "First, Ten." *Seth Godin* (blog), April 2, 2009. https://seths.blog/2009/04/first-ten/.

- Grace Eleyae. "Grace Eleyae -Modern Hair Protection That Actually Works." 2021, https://www.graceeleyae.com/.

- McPeak, Alex. "Grace Eleyae: Journey Towards Creating Fashion-forward Protective Hair Accessories." *Klaviayo* (blog). February 18, 2021. https://www.klaviyo.com/blog/direct-to-consumer-marketing-stories-grace-eleyae.

CHAPTER 11: DEVELOP YOUR FLYWHEEL

- Adams, Tim. "Black Sands Entertainment's Manuel Godoy Reflects on Running a Black-Owned Comic Publisher." *Comic Book Resources* (blog), January 25, 2021. https://www.cbr.com/black-sands-entertainment-manuel-godoy-interview/.

- Collins, Jim. *Good to Great: Why Some Companies Make the Leap...And Others Don't.* New York: Harper Business, 2001.

- Collins, Jim. *Turning the Flywheel: A Monograph to Accompany Good to Great.* New York: Harper Business, 2019.

CHAPTER 12: DON'T BE AFRAID TO FUND YOURSELF

- Lavingia, Sahil. *The Minimalist Entrepreneur: How Great Founders Do More With Less.* New York: Portfolio, 2021.

CHAPTER 13: WHAT IT TAKES TO WIN

- Lafley, A. G., and Roger L. Martin. 2013. *Playing to Win: How Strategy Really Works*. Boston, MA: Harvard Business Review Press, 2013.

- Wodtke, Christina. *Radical focus: Achieving your most important goals with objectives and key results*. Palo Alto: Cucina Media, 2021.

CHAPTER 15: ALWAYS BE LEARNING

- Jorgenson, Eric. "Education." *The Alamanack of Naval Ravikant- A Guide To Wealth and Happiness* (Secret Section). https://www.navalmanack.com/secret-sections/education

- Jorgenson, Eric. *The Alamanack of Naval Ravikant- A Guide To Wealth and Happiness*. Magrathea Publishing, 2020.

- Weiner, Yitzi. "How Zephrine Hanson Of Hampden Farms Is Helping To Address The Growing Challenge Of Food Insecurity." *Social Impact Heroes* (blog). April 21, 2022. http://socialimpactheroes.com/how-zephrine-hanson-of-hampden-farms-is-helping-to-address-the-growing-challenge-of-food-insecurity/.

CONCLUSION: THE TALENTED TENTH

- Godin, Seth. *Purple Cow, New Edition: Transform Your Business by Being Remarkable*. New York: Portfolio, 2009.